PASSIVE INCOME IDEAS AND FINANCIAL FREEDOM INVESTING

How To Never Be Broke, And Make $10,000/Month In Passive Incomes: Affiliat Marketing, Blogging, Stocks, Bonds, Day Trading

Passive Income Ideas: Latest Reliable & Profitable Business Ideas

Make $10,000/month with Affiliate Marketing, Blogging, Dropshipping, Amazon FBA, and More

© Copyright 2019 – All rights reserved

The following eBook is reproduced below with the goal of providing information that is as accurate and reliable as possible. Regardless, purchasing this eBook can be seen as consent to the fact that both the publisher and the author of this book are in no way experts on the topics discussed within and that any recommendations or suggestions that are made herein are for entertainment purposes only. Professionals should be consulted as needed prior to undertaking any of the action endorsed herein.

This declaration is deemed fair and valid by both the American Bar Association and the Committee of Publishers Association and is legally binding throughout the United States.

Furthermore, the transmission, duplication, or reproduction of any of the following work including specific information will be considered an illegal act irrespective of if it is done electronically or in print. This extends to creating a secondary or tertiary copy of the work or a recorded copy and is only allowed with express written consent from the Publisher. All additional right reserved.

The information in the following pages is broadly considered to be a truthful and accurate account of facts and as such any inattention, use or misuse of the information in question by the reader will render any resulting actions solely under this purview. There are no scenarios in which the publisher or the original author of this work can be in any fashion deemed liable for any hardship or damages that may befall them after undertaking information described herein

Additionally, the information in the following pages is intended only for informational purposes and should thus be thought of as universal. As befitting its nature, it is presented without assurance regarding its prolonged validity or interim quality. Trademarks that are mentioned are done without written consent and can in no way be considered an endorsement from the trademark holder.

Table of Contents

INTRODUCTION 7

CHAPTER 1—A BEGINNER'S PASSIVE INCOME 10
FOUR TYPES OF PASSIVE INCOME 11
FIVE QUICK-START STEPS FOR PASSIVE INCOME 14
FIVE GENIUS MICRO-INVESTING TOOLS 22

CHAPTER 2--DISCOVER SELF-PUBLISHING SUCCESS 27
HOW TO WRITE A BOOK. YOUR ROAD TOWARD MAKING BIG BUCKS IN SELF-PUBLISHING 30
MARKETING YOUR BOOK. TIPS FOR MAXIMIZING YOUR BOOK PROFITS 40
TIPS FOR PUBLISHING AUDIO BOOKS 42
SIX STEPS TOWARD EARNING EXTRA INCOME BY PUBLISHING ONLINE COURSES 45

CHAPTER 3--BLOGGING FOR BIG PROFITS 51
THE TRUTH ABOUT EARNING THROUGH BLOGS 51
SEVEN WAYS TO EARN INCOME FROM BLOGGING 57

CHAPTER 4—MAKE PASSIVE INCOME ON THE INTERNET NOW 62
ALL YOU NEED TO KNOW ABOUT AFFILIATE MARKETING 62
FIVE STEPS TOWARD BECOMING AN AFFILIATE MARKETER 64
MAKE MONEY DROPSHIPPING 70
FIVE ESSENTIAL STEPS IN CREATING DROPSHIPPING BUSINESS 72

CHAPTER 5—GET RICHER WHILE YOU SLEEP 75

AMAZON FBA 75
ALL YOU NEED TO KNOW ABOUT PEER-TO-PEER LENDING
OPPORTUNITIES 77
40 WAYS YOU CAN USE YOUR SKILLS OR INTERESTS TO EARN
PASSIVE INCOME 80

CHAPTER 6--MAKE KILLER INVESTMENTS 88

HOW TO START INVESTING IN STOCKS 88
ALL ABOUT CD LADDERING 93
FOUR SIMPLE WAYS TO MAKE REAL ESTATE INVESTMENT INCOME 94

CONCLUSION 98

Introduction

Let's look into some reasons why you're interested in finding some additional income streams. Maybe you already have a job, but the money you earn from that job never seems to provide enough income to meet all your wants and needs. Or maybe you're making enough income to fulfill your current wants and needs, but you can't imagine working the job you're working now forever. You'd like to transition into a career or careers which offer you more independence, more flexibility, more income, or all of the above. Or maybe you're looking for a way to supplement your current income without spending a lot of time to do so. You're not necessarily looking for "easy money", but it would be nice if you could supplement your income without having to allocate a lot of time to do so.

In this book, I'm going to provide you with the information you'll need to create additional income streams for yourself without having to spend a lot of extra time to do so. You may have heard people boast about making money while they sleep. Well, passive income streams can allow you to do exactly that—make money while you are sleeping. Yes, there will be some initial effort required, but I'll show you some ways to make additional income with minimal effort. In some instances, you'll be able to use your money to make more money. On the other hand, if you don't have the money required to make more money, I'll show you some other ways you can increase your income streams with little or no financial investment. So, if you have the money to make more money, but not the time, I can help you. Likewise, if you have the time but not the money to make more money, I can help you.

My name is David Allen. I call myself a "side hustle" expert. For years, I researched and tried many different ways to create additional income for myself and my family. I've made it my mission in life to find easy and practical ways to make additional income. During my journey, I've developed some tried and true ways for people to make extra income. And yes, I've made some mistakes along the way. But I'm always happy to have others learn from my mistakes and missteps. As I grew older, I've found that my mistakes are fewer and further in between. I'm now at a point where I think I have a lot of good information to share with others. I've proven that I can set up some great passive income streams, many of which require very little time and effort.

In the past, I've imparted many of my findings to friends who were eager to learn how to make more passive income. Many of those friends have benefitted substantially from my knowledge and experience in setting up their own passive income streams. Some of them even credit me for changing their lives; many of them have often encouraged me to write this book and share my vast knowledge with others who are looking to improve their own financial status. I'm hoping that you'll be one of the people who benefit immensely from my knowledge and expertise.

With the information I provide, you will be able to create additional income streams for yourself. You'll be able to earn or save extra money immediately with some of the ideas I provide. Other income streams may take slightly longer, but for the most part, you should be able to start earning extra income without spending a lot of time working on it. As you read this book, you'll note that there are many different means of earning additional income. You'll have to determine which of these income streams will work for you. And once you determine that, you will be well on your way toward earning some additional income through the many different streams available to you.

Since you're reading this book, I'm assuming that you'd probably like to start earning extra income sooner than later. With this in mind, I encourage you to start to change your life now by implementing some of the tips and techniques I'm offering. In writing a self-help book like this, there's always the danger that the reader will subscribe to the ideas offered, but then resolve to implement them later. As we all know, many times, people who resolve to implement the changes later will place the ideas on the back burner and then never get back to them. With this in mind, I'd like to encourage you to start implementing these ideas today. After all, why wait to make changes which will allow you to earn additional income and set you on the road to financial independence? Unless you're independently wealthy, I'm sure you'll be happy to start earning some extra income immediately.

The tips and techniques I provide can yield incredible results, if only you'll take the time to implement them. Every chapter in this book should help you in your efforts to create additional income streams without spending a lot of time in implementing or maintaining these streams. By the time you finish reading this book, you'll know all about passive income streams and how they can change your life. Together, we can make it happen.

Chapter 1—A Beginner's Passive Income

Before I can start telling you how you might start earning passive income, I'd like to first define the term "passive income" and tell you how it is different from other forms of income.

Some of you may have heard the mantra, "Make Money While You Sleep". This concept is often paralleled with the concept of passive income.

Passive income is income resulting from cash flow received on a regular basis—with little or no effort or participation on the part of the recipient. Although I wouldn't classify passive income as "easy money", I'll point out that many passive income streams offer opportunities for people to make money without a lot of effort. Yes, some effort may be required at the outset of any passive income opportunity. However, after that initial effort, many passive income streams allow the recipients to derive income on a continuous basis without a lot of participation, effort, or maintenance.

The U.S. Internal Revenue Service lists three categories of income: active income, passive income, and portfolio income. I'll offer a brief description of each income category so we can keyhole the passive income category we'll be focusing on in this book.

Active income is the income a person earns from standard jobs or a mainstream career. If you're a restaurant waiter, a marketing executive, a nurse, or a teacher...any standard career, the salary you earn in doing that job is considered active income. It's called active income because you are active at earning that income. For example, if you are a restaurant waiter, and you decide not to go to work for a couple of weeks, it's likely that you won't get paid or won't derive any income from that job. You'll only earn income from the job if you are active at it.

You may have heard people previously refer to their main jobs as their "A" jobs and their side venture or side hustle jobs as their "B" jobs. When people refer to their "A" jobs, they are almost always referring to active income jobs in which they derive a steady income resulting from their participation in that career. And many people use the income from their "A" job to get into the two other categories of income—passive income and portfolio income.

Portfolio income is income derived from activities such as investments, dividends, interest, capital gains, and royalties. Portfolio income is not earned through regular business activity. Portfolio income is not derived from passive income investments and is not earned through regular business activity.

Passive income, the type of income we'll be focusing on with this book, is income that is derived regularly from activities that require little or no effort or participation on the part of the recipient. As I've already pointed out, passive income isn't always "easy money" or "money made while sleeping", as many passive income activities require at least some initial effort on the behalf of the person who hopes to benefit. And many passive income activities require some ongoing maintenance to remain successful.

Four Types of Passive Income

Before we start telling you some ways you can earn passive income, let's explain the four types of passive income activities, how they work, and how they are different from each other. Here are the four types of passive income activities:

Passive Income Ideas

1) Use Cash to Buy Cash-Flowing Assets. This is the "use money to make money" approach. Now, before you get discouraged, we realize that not all of you have the money required to participate in this option. For those of you that don't, other very viable options which don't require cash will follow. But for those of you that have money to use in increasing your assets, you'll be able to do things such as real estate investments, dividend investing, and business lending to increase your passive income earnings. That said, many people who have the "money to make money" find that they don't have the time to put their money to work for them. With this in mind, I'll provide you with some recommendations on how you can use your money to make more money without allocating a lot of extra time to do so.

2) Build Cash-Flowing Assets. If you don't have mountains of investable cash available, don't despair. You're not alone. You can still build your passive income earnings. Many people have increased their passive income earnings, spending little or no money. Some have built digital products or websites. Others have developed blogs, comparison shopping concepts, affiliate marketing concepts, or even online teaching courses to create ongoing income streams. Although most of these activities require some initial time and effort, they can provide income streams that will last for a long time, without any upfront expenditures.

3) Sell or Share Assets. Do you have assets that you own or control that you can turn into passive income streams? If you'll look around, you can probably identify some tangible assets that could be sold or shared to produce additional income. For example, do you have an exercise bike that you're no longer using and it's just taking up space in your garage? That's an item you could probably sell to earn some extra income. Do you have a car and some extra time to drive around? If so, you can earn some passive income by becoming an Uber or a Lyft driver. Did you collect baseball cards as a kid? Maybe it's time to sell those cards. Do you have an extra bedroom in your house? Maybe you could rent out that extra room. Do you have an empty shed on your property? Maybe you could rent this shed out as a storage space. In all likelihood, you already have assets there that can be turned into cash. Look around and see what assets you already own or control. You'll almost certainly find that some of these assets can be turned into passive income streams.

4) Reverse Passive Income. With this passive income activity, you'll be saving money instead of making money. You'll do so by reducing your ongoing expenses. For example, you could reduce your cable TV bill by renegotiating it or having a negotiating service do that for you. Even if you only negotiate a savings of $20 per month, that will amount to $240 annually. You could also negotiate interest rates on credit cards or switch to credit cards that have better rates or attractive introductory offers. If you are storing some of your belongings in a storage facility, can you get rid of some of the contents of that unit so you can then rent a smaller, less expensive unit? You get the picture…look at your monthly expenses and see if there is a way you could reduce some of those expenses to save money. That's reverse passive income. And even though this activity will not make you more money, it will allow you to save some money that can certainly be used to make more money.

Five Quick-Start Steps for Passive Income

We're going to get going with some ideas for you to start making some quick passive income. Most of the following ideas are offered with the idea that they'll not require a lot of initial startup or setup time. Ideas on more time-intensive passive income streams will follow later in this book. My goal is to get you started immediately with some passive income streams that require very little time. Then, once you realize that you can indeed derive income from these streams, you can proceed to more complex streams that require more startup time.

1)   Credit Cards. As most people have credit cards, and many of those people use credit cards for their ongoing purchases, let's start with how you can derive passive income from your credit cards.

There are a number of things you can do with your credit cards to ensure that you get the maximum passive income from those cards.

The first thing you should consider is the charges that accompany your credit cards. This includes annual fees and interest rates. It's my feeling that you should never pay an annual fee for a credit card that you are using on a regular basis unless the benefits and rewards you receive from having that card substantially outweigh the annual fee. Annual credit card fees will range from $25 to $500 per card. There are plenty credit cards out there that advertise no annual fees and if your credit card company is charging you an annual fee, I suggest that you either consider a switch to another credit card company or call your current credit card company and ask them to waive your annual fee. You should know that almost all credit card companies are open to waiving the annual fees, especially for the first year.

Next, you should find out what the interest rates are on your credit cards and then compare your rate with the rates offered by other credit card companies. If you pay off the full balance on your card every month, the interest rate you get on your card won't matter much, however if you have a continuous balance on that card that you're not able to pay off completely every month, then your interest rate should be a major consideration and you should compare your existing rate with rates offered by other cards. There are many sites on the internet that compare credit card rates, and you should be able to easily compare your rates with other rates with the simple click of a mouse. Again, if your current interest rate is not to your liking but you like your credit card company, you should consider calling your credit card company and asking them to reduce your rate to a more competitive level. Yes, it's possible that they might not accommodate your request, but the worst that can happen is that they say "no". Then if your card rate is not competitive, you can consider switching credit card companies.

Another consideration with credit cards is the benefits or rewards you receive with your card. Does your card offer a cashback program? If so, what is the cashback percentage rate and how does that compare to other cards? Or do you have a travel rewards card? If you do, make sure you plan to utilize the travel miles that are accumulating, before they expire. I've known people who have credit cards with travel rewards that are no longer travelers. For these people, they would be better suited to a credit card that offers rewards other than travel miles. Some credit cards offer gift cards as rewards. Again, you should compare those cards with other cashback or gift card rewards to make sure your credit card company is competitive. If not, consider a switch to another credit card company.

2) **Rewards Programs.** Another way to enhance your earning power is to enroll in rewards programs at places where you regularly

shop. For example, my supermarket chain has a rewards program in which I receive periodic discounts on items I purchase and regular discounts on gas purchases at their service station. When I enrolled in this program, I registered online in less than five minutes. I don't have to carry a plastic card in my wallet; I just give them my phone number whenever I make a purchase. On average, I save 20 to 30 cents per gallon at their service station every time I refuel my car. In a similar vein, I buy office supplies for my small business at Office Max, and they also have a rewards program in which all I have to do is give them my phone number whenever I make a purchase. This rewards program accumulates cash rewards that I can use for future purchases.

Also, there are apps such as Drop, which allow people to earn discounts from their top five retailers. You get to choose your favorite retailers and then you accumulate rewards points with each purchase you make from these five retailers. (Even Lyft and Uber are among the businesses you can choose among your five favorites.) The reward points you accumulate can eventually be redeemed as gift cards from major retailers including Amazon, Starbucks, Groupon, etc. Again, registration is simple and free. You'll be registering retailers that you already purchase from, so it's a can't-lose proposition.

3) Savings Accounts, Checking Accounts. Most people have checking accounts and some people have savings accounts. With all of your bank accounts, I suggest that you verify what your interest rates are for those accounts and then compare them with the rates you might receive from other banks. Again, we have to understand that many people choose their banks for convenience reasons. So if the competing banks' interest rates are only slightly higher than that of your bank's, these higher rates may not merit a switch. However, if they are substantially higher, then you might consider a switch or contact your current bank and ask them if they have any other programs that can be made available to you to raise the rates you're receiving. Please know that interest rates on checking accounts are seldom high and you're probably not going to get rich by trying to negotiate rates or switching to another bank. Nevertheless, "a penny saved is a penny earned" and you can decide if a switch or negotiation is worth it.

Just as important in considering your banking expenses are the fees that you'll pay from your bank. As we all know, banks are well-known for fees that are a major source of their revenue and some banks have even been accused of gouging customers with their fees. In evaluating your bank, I strongly suggest that you analyze the fees they charge. Each bank should be able to supply you with a list of fees. Those fees may even be posted on the bank's website. Does your checking account have a monthly maintenance fee? Is there a minimum balance amount before fees are applied? Do you ever have overdrafts? If so, what are their charges? Many banks have overdraft protection programs they can offer you. Many people take these bank charges for granted when it would behoove them to review these charges at least annually to make sure they are competitive with charges and fees from other banks.

Although reviewing, shopping, or negotiating bank fees may not be the most exciting way to make money and may not make you a millionaire, it is something easy that you can do in very little time to make or save you money on a monthly basis.

4) **Certificates of Deposit.** If you're fortunate enough to have enough money to maintain certificates of deposit, I suggest you "shop" interest rates with banks before depositing funds or renewing certificates. As certificates of deposit don't require much attention, it is not unusual for certificate holders to use banks other than their regular banks. Convenience for certificates of deposit is not a factor that it is for checking accounts, as you basically deposit the funds for your certificates of deposit and then the money just stays in the bank for the term of the certificate. So, don't hesitate to shop interest rates with your certificates of deposit.

5) **Rent Your Assets.** Most of us have at least some rentable assets from which we could derive passive income. Do you have a car? A boat? A vacation home? A recreational vehicle? An empty shed or garage stall? A spare room in your home? All of these assets could provide some passive income streams.

a) **Your house or your spare room.** If you're willing to rent out your house or even a spare room in your house, you can make some serious cash. Airbnb and other similar sites provide reliable vehicles for you to rent out your home. I have friends in Minneapolis that rented out their home for Super Bowl week and, in doing so, they earned enough money to pay their mortgage for an entire year. They earned five figures per night. Yes, they have a nice home, but this will give you an idea of how much money can be raised in renting a house or even a spare room.

Now, it's important to remember that the Super Bowl brings over 100,000 visitors to town and there are not enough hotel rooms to accommodate all the visitors. So, the market is ripe for the picking during that time. Companies like Airbnb will do the background checks on your guests and they will also collect the rental fee you have requested. So, there is very little work on your part except to prepare the home for visitors. My friends who rented out their home for the

Super Bowl made arrangements to stay with relatives during the week they had their house rented.

I have another group of friends that similarly rented out their home in a suburb of Minneapolis for the Ryder Cup golf event, which is an international golf event that is extremely popular, almost as popular as the Super Bowl. Likewise, they were able to pay an entire year's mortgage by renting their house to the family of one of the professional golfers participating in the event. Again, what you can rent your home for will depend on the quality of your home and the popularity of the event in your area, but there is substantial money to be made in renting out your home to visitors, whether they are in your city for a major sporting event, a major concert event, a major political convention, etc. Another Minnesota friend of mine rented out his apartment to a member of the news media who was attending the Republican Convention in nearby St. Paul. Again, there were no hotel rooms available and my friend's apartment was on a light-rail train route with easy access to the convention center in St. Paul where the event was being held.

Do you have a vacation home that sits empty for most of the year? I have a lake home on a secluded lake in northern Minnesota. I use that lake home only about five weeks out of every year. With this in mind, I have started renting out this lake home to interested parties. I, of course, block out the periods in which I am going to be using the lake home, but the home is open for rental at all other times. I used a third-party service to manage my bookings, to correspond with the guests, and to do the cleanings before the guests arrive and after they leave. My participation in the entire activity is mostly centered around accepting the money which the management company collects. (Yes, it's a tough job, but someone has to do it!) I've found this to be an extremely profitable side venture and I've noticed that I have a smile on my face every time I deposit one of the checks from this activity.

One more thought on a far more basic level: If you have a spare bedroom or bedrooms in your home that is mostly being used as a junk room, you might consider renting out this room on either a temporary or an ongoing basis. If you do this, you should obviously make sure you vet or do a background check on your prospective renter. You won't want to grant access to your house to a complete stranger. But if you can find a trustworthy person to rent your spare room, it may well be worth the additional income you'll derive from this passive income activity. As an example, I have a family member who has a small spare bedroom in his family's home. They cleaned all of the junk out of their spare bedroom and rented it to a college kid who had a summer internship in their city. Since it was a small bedroom and since their renter was a cash-strapped college kid, the renters didn't get rich from renting the spare bedroom. Nonetheless, they earned some extra income which they appreciated and they convinced the college kid to mow the lawn in the months he was renting.

b) **Your boat or your recreational vehicle.** Along the same lines, if you own a boat or a recreational vehicle (RV), you're probably not using the boat or the RV on a continual basis. In fact, most boat and RV owners use those items only a couple of times a year. These are expensive assets that can be turned into passive revenue streams. Companies such as Boatsetter and GetMyBoat are vehicles in which you can rent out your boat. Companies such as RVShare and Outdoorsy are available for peer-to-peer RV rentals. If you'll browse those sites, you will get a good idea of how much you can rent your boat or RV for. Your boat rental fee will depend on a number of factors, including how large it is and where it is located. Your RV rental fee will depend on similar factors. It is not unusual for an RV rental to bring a $150 to $300 rental per day. Again, the companies that are in this boat rental or RV rental business will often provide the insurance on the boat or the vehicle. At the same time, they will do background checks on the prospective renters and they will collect the rental fee. They'll then take their cut of the action and pay you the remaining amount.

c)   **Your car.** The average vehicle sits idle for 22 hours a day. Many families own more than one car. Cars are another asset which you can use to make passive income. Companies such as Turo and Getaround offer peer-to-peer car rental platforms. These companies allow you to set the rental price for your vehicle and, importantly, they handle the vetting for the people who want to rent your car and they also handle the insurance for these rentals.

Another way to use your car as an income stream is to become a driver in your spare time. Most of you are familiar with well-known enterprises such as Uber or Lyft. With these companies, it is a relatively simple process to become accepted as one of their drivers and they offer you the flexibility of driving only when you have the spare time to drive. It's a good way to make extra cash. I have friends who are Uber or Lyft drivers in their spare time and they then use the money they earn to make their monthly car payments or their car insurance payments.

Finally, if you're not picky about what your car looks like, you can opt to make it a mobile billboard. Companies like Wrapify will pay you to use your car as a mobile billboard and to advertise various products or services. The money you make in doing this will depend on where you live (highly-populated areas are preferred) and how many miles you drive. Wrapify and other companies like it will track your mileage and then pay you accordingly. It's not unheard of for people to make $100 a week for their mobile billboards.

Five Genius Micro-Investing Tools

I'll admit that until a couple of years ago, I didn't even know what micro-investing was. For those of you who are not familiar with the concept, I'll give you a quick lesson in what it is and how it works. Micro-investing is an activity in which people can invest small amounts in stock. Micro-investing almost always occurs through mobile platforms or apps. Unlike traditional modes of stock investing, micro-investing is not restricted to people who have lots of money. Investments are often very minimal, as the name micro indicates, and investors can usually invest with as little as $1 to $5 at a time. Micro-investing is designed to remove the traditional roadblocks to investing by beginning investors, including brokerage minimums.

With micro-investing, you will not need to become a stock market wonk. As a matter of fact, you won't need to know anything about the stock market. Most of the micro-investing apps will select portfolios for you, based on your preferences, and then they'll place the small amounts you're investing into those funds. When you first start on a micro-investing app, they'll ask you to fill out a questionnaire so they can determine your preferences and then cater your investments toward your preferences.

One thing I really like about many of the micro-investing apps is that they have automatic means for you to make your small investments.

Some of those means are described below under the descriptions of the individual apps.

Although no one would say that you'll become a multi-millionaire by micro-investing and no one would ever proport that you'll become the next Warren Buffett, micro-investing is a good way to get your feet wet in the stock market without laying out or risking a lot of cash. You'll be able to make or save small amounts of money without a major cash outlay and without broker's minimums and fees.

As you might imagine, there are quite a few micro-investing apps to choose from. I'll outline a few of these apps below, but you should note that there are always new apps coming out that you may want to look into if you are interested in micro-investing.

1) **Acorns.** This is one of the most popular apps, as it allows you to invest very small amounts by automatically rounding your debit and credit card charges to the nearest higher dollar amount and then it invests this small extra amount (always less than $1) for you. For example, if I buy a toner cartridge for my printer and the cost of that cartridge is $24.39, Acorns will round the charge up to $25 and add the 61 cents change to my investment account. If for whatever reason, you don't want these amounts invested automatically, you can manually select for which charges these small extra amounts can be invested. The thing I like about this site automatically rounding my charges to the next highest dollar amount is that I consider these small amounts to be pocket change which will have very little impact on my bank account and which I'm never going to miss. But with all the debit

and credit charges I make, those small amounts add up to a decent investment account over a period of time.

To give you an idea as to the amount of money I can save and invest with the Acorns app, I've been averaging over $40 per month saved and invested. Admittedly, I use my debit and credit cards quite frequently, because I use them for personal purchases and for my small business purchases (and I rarely pay cash for the items I purchase), but this will give you an idea as to what you might expect to earn on the Acorns app. I project that my annual savings/investments will total somewhere between $450 and $500 annually. No, that won't put me in the same tax category as Amazon founder Jeff Bezos, but $500 isn't chump change either, at least not for me.

Acorns charges $1 a month for its services, money that I easily get back from my investments. As mentioned before, they'll ask you a few questions when you register with them and they'll use the information you provide to create a financial profile for you. They'll then build your investment portfolio, which can range from conservative to aggressive, depending on the information you give them on your questionnaire.

2) **Stash.** Stash is a bit different than Acorns, as it is slightly more hands-on for investors. With this app, instead of adding to your debit and credit card charges, Stash is set up so you can withdraw a specified amount from your bank account each week or each month. Like Acorns, Stash will ask you a set of questions in an effort to determine whether they should steer you toward conservative, moderate, or aggressive investments. Once they have determined this, they will provide you with a set of simple portfolios in which you can choose to invest. Again, you'll not need to be a stock expert to determine which stocks you'll invest in, but you'll at least be required to choose a preference, something you won't have to do with Acorns. Stash has a $1 monthly fee and they require that you've accumulated a minimum of $5 before you can start investing.

3)   **Rize.** Rize is a goal-oriented savings and investment app. The savings component of this app is designed to help you save the amounts of money you want in order to pay for things you want. For example, if you want to get a new surfboard at a cost of about $400, Rize will set you up on a savings program in which they will designate a specified amount of each of your paychecks toward this purchase. (You'll be the one who specifies the amount to be deducted from each paycheck.) At the same time, you tell them how much money you'll need to purchase a new surfboard, you'll also tell them when you'd like to have this surfboard. With this app, you can easily adjust your settings at any time. You can accelerate or decelerate your payments, if necessary. Rize charges an annual management fee of 0.25% on your investments. Some of these fees are offset by the 1.6% interest they pay on your balance.

4)   **Robinhood.** The Robinhood app is an app for buying and selling stocks on U.S. exchanges. The app can also be used to buy and sell ETFs (exchange-traded funds) and cryptocurrencies. This program is well-known because it is free and it doesn't charge any of the fees that are typically associated with stock transactions. No commissions, no account maintenance fees, no trading fees. On the other hand, the Robinhood app is a bare-bones app which does not offer investment advice or research. If you're interested in buying or selling stocks on this app, you'll have to get your advice elsewhere.

5) Betterment. Unlike Robinhood, Betterment allows you to be hands-off with your investments. It also gives you access to financial advisors who can offer investment advice through the app's messaging system. Betterment has two tiers: The Betterment Digital tier is available with no required account minimum. Betterment charges 0.25% of assets for its Digital tier. The company also offers Betterment Premium at 0.40% of assets with a minimum investment of $100,000. With Betterment Premium, the company offers unlimited phone access to members. I realize that Betterment Premium will not be viable to most of us here, but the Betterment Digital tier is a good deal if you are interested to buy and sell stocks and to be able to solicit the advice of their financial advisors throughout the process.

Chapter 2--Discover Self-Publishing Success

Self-publishing is one of the most popular forms of earning passive income. Before I tell you how to discover self-publishing success, I want to make sure you understand what self-publishing is. In the days before the internet, if you wanted to write a book and have it published, you were either totally at the discretion of traditional publishers or you had to pay to have large quantities of your own book printed. Authors who wanted to have their own books printed, probably because they couldn't sell them to publishers, often had to purchase as many as 5000 books in order to get a reasonable price.

In those days, a friend of mine who eventually became a New York Times best-selling author had always had the dream to be an author. After he finished writing his first book, he submitted it to 27 different publishers. He received 27 letters of rejection. He believed in his book and his writing abilities so sincerely that he decided to go the "vanity press" route and have his book printed without a publisher. He had to print 5000 books at that time, and, as a student recently out of college and a person who held a bartending job to pay the bills, he didn't have anything close to the money he needed to print the 5000-book minimum. He was a great salesman and he eventually secured the funds needed through loans from some of his bar patrons.

He had the 5000 books printed and then loaded up the trunk of his car with boxes of his books and drove from bookstore to bookstore in an effort to hawk his books. As I mentioned before, he was a great salesman and he was eventually able to sell all 5000 of his political thriller books to bookstores and individuals. Soon after he reordered his second batch of books, he received a call from a publisher who had been tracking his book purchases from the "vanity press". That publisher asked him to submit a manuscript and soon after that, my friend was offered his first book contract from a publisher. He went on to make a career of it and he wrote six New York Times bestsellers before he, unfortunately, died of cancer at an early age.

I tell you this story of how things used to be so I can illustrate how things have changed since the advent of the internet and digital printers. Now you can write a book, you can load it to an online self-publishing site, and you can sell digital books, printed books, or audiobooks. Most impressively, you can purchase printed books in minimum quantities of one. Yes, you read that right. You can have one book printed at a time. As a matter of fact, with digital printers, your printed book will not be printed until someone orders it online. Then the printer will ship that book within a matter of days, instead of the matter of weeks or months required for printing in the days before the internet.

Although there are quite a few steps involved in writing and self-publishing a book, the process is now so much easier than it ever was before and it can be done very inexpensively. In this book chapter, I'm going to tell you how to write and publish your own books. Publishing your own books is one of the most popular ways for people to earn passive income.

There are a ton of success stories about people who have made a fortune through self-publishing their own books.

Accurate statistics on the book industry aren't always easy to find, but I have some statistics that will show you what a huge market the book market is. According to the NPD Group (National Purchase Diary), a well-known American market research firm, over 696 million printed books were sold in 2018. According to Data Guy, a renowned book industry analyst, over 781 million eBooks were sold from April 2017 through September 2018, totaling a sales amount of $4.02 billion. This should give you a good idea of what you'll be getting into when you decide to self-publish books.

Before we get further along, I should probably define eBooks for those of you who may not be quite sure what the term encompasses. The term eBook is short for electronic book, and it includes all books that can be read on mobile devices such as cell phones and tablets, computers, and eBook devices such as Kindle and Nook.

When you self-publish your books, you are going to have to decide if you want printed books, ebooks, audiobooks, or all of the above. It's very common now for people to publish printed and eBook versions of the same book. Audiobooks are not quite as popular, but they are quickly rising in popularity and they offer yet another vehicle for you to get your book out there for people who prefer listening to books instead of reading them.

Probably the biggest success story in e-publishing is the story of author E.L. James and her *50 Shades of Gray* series. She published her first book in that series in 2011 as an eBook and a print-on-demand paperback. Her books have now sold over a million copies, including books that have now been turned into movies.

Self-publishing success stories are abundant on the internet. I'll take the time to give you one woman's story because it's a great success story and it will give you an idea of the possibilities that self-publishing can offer. Admittedly, very few people will ever achieve these lofty levels, but it's nice to dream, isn't it? Amanda Hocking was an unknown author from Minnesota who couldn't get published by a traditional publisher. She worked a day job as a group home caregiver to pay the bills and then wrote paranormal novels in her spare time. Eventually, she had written 17 books and had a tall pile of rejection letters from publishers and agents, who either didn't believe in her talents or didn't believe that there would be much interest in the genre. Finally, in 2010, frustrated by the publishers and agents who kept rejecting her, Amanda decided to see if she could sell her books on Amazon's Kindle. She self-published her vampire novel, *My Blood Approves,* on Amazon's site. She soon started selling nine books a week on the site. No great shakes, of course, but at least there was some interest, enough interest to prompt her to self-publish three additional books in the series on the site. It wasn't long after posting those three additional books that the series took off. Word obviously got around and from April 2010 through March 2011, she sold over a million copies of nine different books and earned $2 million in sales for those books. At one point, she was selling an average of 9000 books a day. Her sales strategy was brilliant. She sold the first books in her series at only 99 cents in an attempt to get her readers hooked on the series. The subsequent books in the series then sold for $2.99. Some of the conventional publishing houses scoffed at the idea of selling a book for only 99 cents, but Amanda Hocking sold such a huge volume of books that her sales soon put those criticisms to rest. Amanda Hocking is a poster child for the potential of self-publishing.

Now that we have some of the general information and some success stories out of the way, let's get into the nitty-gritty of how to write and publish a book.

How to Write A Book. Your Road Toward Making Big Bucks in Self-Publishing

Find a topic. Before you can write a book, you are going to have to select a subject or a topic. I suggest that you start out with a project that you are interested in. If you can find a topic or niche in which you are interested or passionate, you'll find that you'll enjoy writing the book a lot more. You'll also find that writing a book about something you are knowledgeable or interested in will require a lot less research.

If you don't have a particular subject or niche in mind and just want to write a book to earn extra income, I suggest that you first examine your personal areas of expertise or interest. For example, I have a friend of mine who is an avid biker (bicycle, not motorcycle). A few years ago, he was telling me how he had ridden on every bike trail in the state of Minnesota. He was telling me which trails he really enjoyed, and which trails he only mildly enjoyed. He even told me all about the ice cream shops or the coffee cafes that he would stop in as he traversed these trails. Many of the trails went through small towns that had interesting things to see or hidden gems, such as antique shops, diners, bakeries, or candy shops.

As he was relaying all of this information to me, I finally said, "You know, you should write a book about that. You're a fountain of information on Minnesota bike trails and I think people would be willing to pay for that information." He was taken aback by my idea and brushed it off by saying, "I could never do that. I'm not an author."

I didn't let the subject die and offered to help him self-publish his book if he was willing to gather all of the information. And I'm happy to say that he did publish a book on Minnesota bike trails. Although this book hasn't made him a millionaire, he enjoyed doing it, he is proud that he did it, and he now receives monthly royalty checks from the sales of his book. As a matter of fact, he now uses his bike book sales to fuel his weekend bike trips.

So the moral of the story for those of you who want to write books to earn some extra income: I suggest that you start with an area in which you are knowledgeable or passionate and then determine how to convey that information in a book. I have a friend who has coached youth sports for much of his adult life. He is also the parent of two boys who love sports. He has written a book for adults on how to coach their kids. Another friend of mine has been a midwife for over 20 years. She wrote a book targeted at expectant mothers. She discussed the benefits of using a midwife and discussed whether expecting parents should use a midwife or a doctor. Both the parent–coach and the midwife conveyed valuable information in their books and they've derived monthly supplementary income from the sales of those books.

In determining a topic for your book or books, don't be discouraged if there are already multiple books available on the subject you're considering. This might be a plus instead of a minus. For example, if you want to write a book on nutrition, you'll quickly note that you'll not be the first person to do so. There are thousands of books out there on nutrition. This should not discourage you, as it shows that there is definitely an interest in the subject. If you can bring a unique perspective to any topic, you'll have a chance to be successful in selling your book.

Develop a Working Title. Jot down ideas for the title of your book as you come up with them. This so-called title will simply be a working title, and you'll be able to change it any time before the book is published. But your working title will serve as a constant reminder of the topic of your book. If you are writing a self-help book, you will certainly want to come up with a title that will entice the reader to buy and read the book. Titles like "How to Lose 10 Pounds in 10 Days" and "How to Train Your New Puppy" will allow prospective buyers and readers to immediately determine if they have further interest in your book.

Develop an Outline. In writing a book, it's going to be important for you to establish some sort of organization with the content of that book. With this in mind, you'll need to develop an outline for the content of that book, possibly even a chapter by chapter outline which you can adhere to in writing the book.

Select a Template for Your Book. Many novice authors find it easier to use a template in writing their books. There are multiple sites on the internet that offer free book templates, including hubspot.com. In some instances, you'll have a number of different templates you can choose from. These templates will help you stay organized throughout the process of writing your book. As you become more accomplished or experienced at writing books, you probably won't need a template. However, it is a valuable tool for beginners.

Write the Book. After you've done all of the above, it's time to get into the nitty-gritty of writing the book itself. This, along with any research which might be required, will probably be the most time-consuming element in making a book. Most experienced authors will set a designated time to write their books, e.g., 2 hours a day, 15 hours a week, etc. They'll also determine which time of the day is best for them to do their writing, e.g., early morning, late evening after the kids have gone to bed, etc.

What if you're not a good writer or what if you have valuable information or a great story to impart to others but don't know how to put it on paper? If this is the case, you're probably going to have to hire someone to write your book for you. Ghostwriters are available on many sites, including Upwork.com. If you're going to hire a freelancer to write your book or your story, I encourage you to remember that they are only going to be able to be as good as the information you provide them with. I've ghostwritten many books and have gathered the information in a number of ways, including a written outline from the person who wants the book written, a collection of blogs by the same person, a weekly one- or two-hour tape-recorded phone interview or Skype interview, etc. Either way, you will have to figure out how to get the necessary information to the freelancer. If you are hiring a freelancer you haven't worked with before, I encourage you to request samples of their writing so you can review the quality and style of their writing and make sure it complies with your expectations. Along the same lines, in working with a freelancer, I suggest that you ask them to write the first chapter of your book for a nominal fee and then proceed with the remainder of the book after you've made sure you're on the right track. This sample chapter will benefit both you and the freelancer, as you'll want to make sure you're "on the same page" before you get too far into the project.

Adding Illustrations, Graphs, Photos. After you've written the book, you should determine whether the addition of illustrations, graphs, or photos will add value to the book. As an example, I just finished writing a book which tells the true story of a former US naval officer who was a Japanese prisoner-of-war in the Philippines in World War II. Although the story itself was incredible, I knew that adding photos to the book would add to the value, as I knew that the readers would want to see the man whose story we told. And even though these were old black-and-white photos and weren't in mint condition, they added value to the book and we opted to include them. A friend of mine recently completed a pie recipe book. Obviously, photos of the pies add a lot to the value of the book, as people who buy recipe books are accustomed to photos of the recipe items. This friend had a limited budget in producing this recipe book, so she opted to take photos of the different pies with her cell phone instead of paying a professional photographer to do so.

Cover Design. Whether you're producing a printed book or an eBook, you should know that how you package that book is likely to be an extremely important factor in the sales of the book. If you've ever browsed books in a bookstore or in the library, you'll know that the cover or jacket of a book can certainly influence whether you buy that book or select that book to read. Packaging is very important. With this in mind, you'll want to create an attractive cover for your book. Unless you are a designer (most of us aren't), you're going to have to hire a freelancer to design your cover. Please know that there are many graphic artists who specialize in designing book covers. I have previously used the fiverr.com site to hire freelancers for my cover designs. I have always been able to hire someone for under $100 to do that and I've been able to get some great designs. Again, with these freelancers, their success may well depend on the instructions you give them. On the Fiverr site, you'll have many freelancers to choose from. In working with them, you have to tell them the size of the book you are looking to produce, whether you want a cover designed for a print book or an eBook or both, and you'll also have to provide the copy that you want on the cover of the book, including the title and a brief description of the book.

In working with freelancers to design covers, I have almost always opted to give them a photo or illustration which I want them to use on the cover. There are a number of stock photo sites on the internet which offer huge selections and excellent search engines for you to find photos or illustrations that you can use on your book covers. I have previously used istockphoto.com for my photo and illustration needs. On this site, I have generally been able to purchase a photograph for under $35 to use on my book covers. These are non-licensed photographs in which the photographers or illustrators post photos or illustrations on the site which are available for purchase on an ongoing basis. The photographers or illustrators than get a cut every time a customer purchases their photo or illustration.

Formatting. Whether you want a printed book, an eBook, or both, your book is going to have to be formatted so it can be properly uploaded to the sites that will print or sell your book. If you have the time, you can certainly learn how to do the formatting yourself through tutorials on the internet. If you don't have the time (most people don't), you can always hire a freelancer to do that for you. Again, fiverr.com offers a wide selection of freelancers who will format your book for prices advertised from $15 to $100. In hiring a freelancer to format your book, you'll again need to give them the size of the book if you're going to have a printed book. You're also going to have to tell them who you plan to use to print or sell your books. In working with freelancers on some sites like the Fiverr site, please remember that these freelancers are from all over the world and there may be time differences or language differences involved. With many of these freelancers, English is a second language, but most of them are quite proficient in English. And most of them have done numerous formatting or cover design projects, so they're likely to know exactly what you will need to submit to various self-publishing platforms.

ISBN. If you're going to have a printed book, you'll need an ISBN. ISBN stands for International Standard Book Number and it is a 13-digit number used by publishers, booksellers, and libraries to identify books. ISBN numbers are not required for eBooks. Purchasing an ISBN is a simple process and there are a number of ISBN sellers on the internet. I use isbnservices.com and paid $18.99 for my most recent ISBN. That ISBN includes a barcode which can be used for scanning by booksellers and libraries.

Determining Your Sell Price. As a self-published author, you can set your own selling price. (If you were using a traditional publisher, they would dictate what price you sell at.) In determining a selling price, I always instruct authors to get on publishing platforms such as Amazon to find out what the books in their genre are selling for. Once you have determined that, you should settle on a selling price which falls somewhere within that range. If you are offering a printed version of the book, your sell price should be printed on the back cover of your book inside the ISBN and bar code area. In determining a price for a printed book, please remember that you should select the highest possible price you would sell the book at and then note that you will be able to discount that book when and if you see fit to do so. For example, I wrote a 250-page memoir for which I decided the maximum sell price would be $16. I set this price not only because it was comparable to the prices of other memoirs, but because I wanted my readers who ordered a printed copy from Amazon to be able to spend $20 or less, including shipping. I then made some personal appearances at book clubs and libraries and bookstores, and, in the case of book clubs and libraries, I was able to discount the book to $12 or $14 if they purchased on the spot. This was attractive to prospective readers as everyone likes a discount and they wouldn't have to pay for shipping as they would if they ordered from an internet source. At the time I was doing that (a few years ago), I was paying somewhere between $3 and $4 per book and buying about 25 to 50 books at a time for my presentations, so you can see that my profit margin was still very good, even when I discounted the book.

Pricing for eBooks is slightly different and prices are usually substantially less because there are no actual printing or materials involved. Most eBooks will sell anywhere from $2.99 to $9.99. If you use the Amazon Kindle Direct Publishing (KDP) platform to sell your book, you can expect royalties of 70% on any books that are sold within that $2.99-$9.99 price range. Anything that falls outside that price range, higher or lower, your royalties will drop to 35%. As you can see by those numbers, Amazon strongly prefers that you sell your eBooks on their platform for $2.99-$9.99. And eBooks are different than printed books in that you can't discount them whenever you see fit. For the most part, the selling price you establish is the price you'll sell the book. That said, you should note that KDP offers prospective readers the opportunity to sample a free chapter to see if they want to buy the book. They also offer a giveaway program in which you can offer your book for free when the book is first posted for sale, in an attempt to create interest for the book. Many authors have used this free offer to successfully promote their book and create subsequent sales from the interest they create.

In determining your price for eBooks, the genre of the book will be very important in determining the price. For example, if it is a romance book for which you are hoping for mass consumption, then you'll note that most of these romance novels are sold at the lower end of the price spectrum. On the other hand, if you have a historical non-fiction book such as the book I mentioned concerning the US naval officer who was a Japanese prisoner-of-war, you can probably get more money for that book, as it is a non-fiction account that is not targeted for mass consumption and will appeal mostly to war veterans and history buffs.

Upload Your Book. Now things start to get exciting. You're ready to roll. Your book is finished and it's time to upload it to the platform or platforms on which you intend to sell it. There are many platforms available for you to use in selling your book. I will outline a few of them here for your convenience, but please remember that there are additional options available to you.

1)   Amazon/Kindle. This is the most well-known platform for selling self-published books. Over two-thirds of all eBook purchases are made through Amazon's Kindle Direct Publishing (KDP), the platform I mentioned in the section immediately preceding this one. If you're serious about selling your book as a passive income stream, Amazon's Kindle platform should be at or near the top of your list. One of the things that make the KDP platform so popular is that your prospective readers can get the Kindle app for their computer, tablet, or phone. This means that it will be easy for them to purchase and read your book. Amazon also has a partnership with Audible which will allow you to easily convert your book to an audio format and sell additional books. I'll go into further detail on audiobooks in the paragraphs that follow. So, one of the big advantages of using the Amazon platform to sell your book is that it is the most popular platform for buying and selling books. Also, it offers you the opportunity to publish digital, printed, and audio versions of your book all in one platform.

2)   Nook. Barnes & Noble is a large book retailer and their e-reader device is called the Nook. The Nook is responsible for about a quarter of all e-readership so this is another platform that you should strongly consider for any book you want to sell. Royalties with the Nook platform are very similar to those of Amazon/Kindle. Nook royalties are 65% of the list price for any books sold between $2.99 and $9.99; 40% for books sold outside that range.

3) **iBooks.** Publishing your book on iBooks will allow you to sell your books in the Apple iBookstore. It means that your book can be made available to anyone that has an iPhone, and IPad, or a Mac, all Apple devices.

4) **Others.** I've outlined the three main platforms above, but you should know that there are also other platforms available for you to use in selling your book. Although I won't go into detail with those other options here, I would at least like to mention a few of them, so you can research yourself if you have further interest. Platforms such as Smashwords, Kobo, and Scribd are also very viable platforms on which to sell books. They might not offer the large numbers that the "big three" platforms do, but they still offer the opportunity for you to sell more books and make more money.

Marketing Your Book. Tips for Maximizing Your Book Profits

Marketing Your Book. Just because you've finished writing your book and posted it for sale on various platforms doesn't mean that you're done. Marketing your book is one of the most crucial factors in making money from your book. A number of years ago, a friend of mine hosted a New Year's Eve party for his friends and co-workers. He purchased large amounts of food and cold beverages for his party, presuming that it would be the party of the year. When the clock struck midnight and the new year rolled in, he asked me what I thought was the reason why only less than a dozen people at his party. "I'm not sure", I responded. "Did you tell people you were having the party?" My friend responded that he had been so busy making party plans that he hadn't had the chance to tell a lot of people about the party. As he himself said, "I thought the word would get around."

Well, the same goes for your book. Now that you've invested time and money to write your book, it's time to tell people that it's available. You can't expect people to buy your book if they don't even know it exists.

With this in mind, I have some tips for you to market your book and sell it. If you want to maximize the extra money you earn from your book, you'll need to market it. And if you can market it successfully, you might be able to reap financial benefits from it for quite some time.

Here are some simple and inexpensive ways you can market your book:

1) **Social Media.** Most of us already have a social media presence. Social media offers you a great opportunity to get the word out about your new book. Authors have used social media platforms such as Facebook, Instagram, Twitter, Tumblr, Reddit, and Pinterest to promote their new books. In many instances, they would offer a free sample for readers in an effort to get them interested to buy the book. Also, please know that you should not just use these platforms once to promote your book. I've used those platforms multiple times, to announce that the book is available, to publish positive reviews I get on the book, to remind people that your book would make a great holiday gift, etc.

2) **Blogs, Websites.** Do you have a blog or a website which you can use to direct visitors to the platforms where they can purchase your book? If so, you should make sure you use these platforms to promote your book. If not, you may want to consider creating a blog to promote your new book and any future books.

3) **Emails, Texts.** I have also used mass emails and texts to announce the availability of my books. Over the years, I've accumulated a substantial address book. All of these people are potential customers. So, whenever I have a new book available, I send a mass email to my contacts, including a sales flyer which shows the cover of the book along with a brief description of the book and where they can purchase the book.

4) **Bookmarks, Postcards.** Also, each time I have a new book out, I print some bookmarks and postcards which I can hand out to people that I meet in person. I don't actually mail many of the postcards, but I like to hand them out to people I meet. I like the size of postcards because they can contain more information than the smaller bookmarks. Bookmarks and postcards are inexpensive ways to promote your book. I think I paid $25 plus shipping for 500 bookmarks and $30 plus shipping for 500 postcards from an online source. I use these items almost like business cards, handing them out readily to just about everyone I meet.

Tips for Publishing Audio Books

The audiobook market is yet another platform for you to use in enhancing your self-published book sales. Although the audiobook market isn't as large as the printed book or eBook market, it is a burgeoning market that merits your consideration. In a day and age where podcasts and radio apps are popular, it is important to note that some people prefer to view or listen to things instead of reading them. Whether they are driving in a car, working out at the health club, or lying on the beach, some people like to listen to audiobooks. And, of course, there are other people who just don't like to read and they prefer audio or visual methods.

I'm of the belief that you should wait to see how successful your printed books or eBooks are before you decide to publish them as audiobooks. The reason I say this is because of the extra time and extra expense involved. Before you invest more time or money in your book, you should first determine if it is successful in printed or eBook format. If so, you should definitely publish your book in audio format. If you don't, you'll be leaving money on the table that you could be earning by using an audio format.

Audiobook Creation Exchange (ACX) is the most popular platform for audiobooks. If you add your audiobook to ACX, it will be available for sale on Amazon, Audible, and the Apple Audio Store. For those of you not familiar with Audible, it is a seller and producer of spoken audio entertainment, information, and educational programming on the internet. It is a top seller of digital audiobooks.

If you publish your book on ACX, you'll earn royalties of 20% to 40% of whatever your sell price is.

Here is some quick general information regarding converting your book from a printed or digital format to an audio format.

1) **Prepare Your Book for Audio.** You'll need to edit your printed or digital books so they can be used as audiobooks. In other words, remove everything that won't make sense in an audio format, i.e., no references to illustrations, photos, or graphs; no hyperlinks or "click here" prompts.

2) Decide Who Will Record Your Audio. If you're going to have an audiobook, you're going to have to determine who will record your book? Will you want to hire a narrator or will you want to record the book in your own voice? If you have an education book or a memoir, you'll be more likely to be the narrator for your own book than you would for a book of fiction in which you may be better served to use someone with an acting skillset. In my own experience, I have always hired a narrator, even for my own memoir. I've done that for a number of reasons, but mostly because I don't have a great narrator's voice. My throat gets dry very quickly when I talk a lot, and I'm sure that it would take me long periods of time to narrate a book so listeners would quickly tire of my raspy voice. Also, I have a relatively noisy home environment, including a lot of street noise, and I am afraid the background noise would be too distracting to the listener. I had thought previously about renting a recording studio to record my book, but I feel that the money I would have spent renting a studio could just as well be spent in paying a narrator.

3) Hiring a Narrator. Hiring a narrator may not be as expensive as you might think. I have an associate who hires narrators on a frequent basis and he is usually able to hire someone for less than $500. He tells me that there are two sites he would recommend in hiring a freelance narrator. Those sites are Upwork and Voices. ACX also has narrators you can hire for your book. In hiring any freelance narrator, you should absolutely ask them to provide previous samples of their work. And, you might also ask them to narrate a small portion of your book before you officially hire them. In this way, you can make sure they are a good fit for your project before you get too far into the book.

4) **Rent a Recording Studio; Narrate Your Own Book.** If you want to narrate your own book, and if your home or office environment is too noisy to do so, you may have to rent a recording studio to use in narrating your book. I have a friend who tells me that this can be a 10- to 20-hour process, depending on the length of your book, so you may have to book the studio for multiple days. Again, beware that using your voice for such a long period of time may affect the quality of your voice, so you might have to rent the studio in smaller blocks of maybe three or four hours at a time.

If you want to learn more about creating an audiobook, I suggest that you visit selfpublishingschool.com, where Chandler Bolt has an extensive article on exactly how to publish an audiobook.

Six Steps Toward Earning Extra Income by Publishing Online Courses

I'd be remiss if I did not discuss how publishing online courses can create additional revenue streams for you. The market for online courses and online learning is getting bigger and bigger. The research firm Global Market Insights projects that online learning courses could reach $240 billion by 2023. That's an astronomical number.

With this in mind, I encourage you to consider developing online courses to create additional passive income streams for yourself. Here are some simple tips to get you started on developing an online course or courses:

1) **Find a topic.** What are you an expert at? Do you have information that is valuable to others…to the point that others will be willing to pay to learn that information? Or, even if you are not an expert, can you become an expert? One of the major success stories in online courses is that of Purna Duggirala, a man from India who goes by the name of Chandoo. A number of years ago, Chandoo recognized an opportunity to make money by hosting online courses. He noticed that people did not properly know how to use the Excel software program, so he came up with a series of courses in which he taught subscribers how to become excellent or awesome at Excel. He made over $1 million in 2014 with that concept. Again, we all know that these success stories only show the top range a person can earn. It's unlikely that you'll earn that kind of cash with your online courses. But again, there's no harm in dreaming. Even if you can garner an additional $500 to $1000 every month from your online course or courses, I'm sure you'd take it.

In determining a topic for your online courses, I suggest that you first take a personal inventory of your own knowledge to see if there is anything you can impart to people who would be willing to pay for your expertise. Are you an expert at technology? Can you teach coding or programming? Do you speak multiple languages? Can you teach one of those languages to people who are planning to visit a foreign country? A friend of mine is originally from the Philippines. Besides now speaking impeccable English, she speaks fluent Visayan and Tagalog, two languages that are spoken by many Filipinos. So, with the ability to speak these languages, she created an online mini-course series in which she teaches English-speaking people who are getting ready to visit the Philippines how to speak those native languages. She has been quite successful in getting people to subscribe to her courses and has derived a nice supplemental income from those courses.

If you don't have any areas where you would consider yourself an expert, you can always become an expert simply by garnering the information you have a passion for and then inserting that information into a course that is available online to others. I read a story about a man who knew nothing about coding, but by the time he finished reading multiple books on the subject, taking some online courses and tutorials, he knew more than almost all of the people who were interested in the same subject. So even though he hadn't started out as an expert, he became an expert with valuable information that people were willing to pay for.

2) Create a course outline. If you're going to create an online course, you'll most certainly need an outline for that course. You'll not only use that outline in conveying information to subscribers, but you'll also use that outline to sell the course to prospective subscribers, who are sure to want to know what the course entails before they enroll in it. In setting up your course, please know that most online courses are limited to a maximum of 20 minutes per session. After that, subscribers start to lose interest. I strongly suggest that you set up a series of 15- to 20-minute courses that can teach people everything they want to know about whatever subject you're teaching. That might entail as few as three-course sessions or as many as 10. Either way, limit your sessions to 20 minutes. And remember, each course should get your subscribers closer to the goals and objectives of your course.

3) Determine the price of your course. In determining a price for your online course, please know that the length of the course should not be the main determinant. First, you should check to see what your competitors in the same subject are selling their courses for. Then, you should look at how your expertise falls within the spectrum of those people who are offering similar courses. For example, if Bill Gates or Paul Allen were to offer a course on how to use Windows, it's safe to assume that you're probably not going to be able to charge the same amount for a similar course. I say that somewhat tongue-in-cheek, but if you're a neophyte in the field for which your offering an online course, you're probably not going to be able to charge as much as an expert in the field. Finally, in determining the price for your online course, you should consider how much value you are giving the course subscriber. For example, if you're going to offer an online course which can be used to make thousands of dollars, you should be able to charge a lot more for that course than you would in offering to teach Portuguese to people who are planning on visiting Brazil. Or if your online course is solving a problem, a course that solves a major problem should obviously be priced higher than a course that solves a minor problem. Use common sense to set your sell price, and don't be afraid to test different price points. It's your course and you should be able to set whatever price you like for that course, as long as people are willing to subscribe.

I'd like to mention one other thing in regards to pricing for online courses. Yes, you'll be able to make money if you can tell people how to do something, but you'll be able to make even more money if you can show them how to do something. And finally, you'll be able to charge even more if you can offer support for the information you are trying to teach. For example, if you have a course on how to self-publish a book, are you available to answer individual questions your subscribers might have.

4) **Create the course content.** Using your course outline, you should create course content for each of your lesson segments. Depending on your own personal preference, you can decide whether you'll want to work from a script or not, but you'll definitely want to work from an outline. Many of the most successful online courses do not work from a script and are more casual and conversational, but almost all of them work from an outline.

5) Create the course. Your next step is to create the course itself. By now, you'll have decided if your course is going to be a written course, an audio course, or a video course. Obviously, video courses are the most successful, because people like to see visuals as they learn. If you're going to do a video course, you won't need to hire a video expert to shoot or edit your lessons. You should be able to do this on your phone, and you should know that there are many easy-to-use tools and software programs available. Programs such as Camtasia and Quicktime are among the programs that can be used for screen recordings.

When you are creating your course, you should remind yourself that it's not realistic to expect your lesson video recording to have the feel of a major television production. The content of the lesson will be more important than the presentation and you will certainly get better at the production of your lessons as you become more experienced at doing so.

6) Launch your course. There are a ton of different platforms available to host your online courses. Instead of trying to go through a multitude of these platforms, I will tell you how one of the most popular platforms works so you can get an idea of what you might expect in publishing and selling the online courses you develop. Udemy.com is the world's largest online learning platform. More than 30 million students have taken courses on Udemy; over 50,000 instructors offer over 130,000 courses in over 60 languages. This will give you an idea of the scope of the Udemy platform. Anyone can post a course on Udemy. If you want to charge a fee to the students on Udemy, you will need to complete a free application which is usually approved within two days. For any students you get to take your course, you will receive 97% of the course fee. Udemy will take a 3% commission. If Udemy secures students for your courses via their own marketing, they will then take a 50% commission amount and the instructor will receive the other 50%. As Udemy does not charge a hosting fee, the only way they make money is by selling courses. Udemy is widely known as a good place to start for the novice online instructors, as it offers a simple way for instructors/sellers to assemble content like PowerPoint slides, PDF documents, and YouTube videos into a coherent course. The Udemy platform also offers a variety of marketing tools to help sellers sell their course.

Other popular online learning course platforms include Teachable, WizIQ, Thinkific, and Ruzuka. If you want to take a more in-depth look at the different online course platforms which are available, I recommend that you visit www.learningrevolution.net/sell-online-courses/, where they have a nice article outlining 15 of the best online learning course platforms.

Whether you're publishing printed books, digital books, audiobooks, or online learning courses, these self-publishing methods offer you some excellent opportunities to create passive income streams which can make you money for long periods of time after you've done the initial work to develop the materials. These self-publishing venues are not 100% passive income, as there is some initial work required. However, once you have published the materials, you should be able to derive additional income for long periods of time—weeks, months, even years—with very little additional work.

Chapter 3--Blogging for Big Profits

Another great way for you to create additional passive income will be for you to create a series of blogs. We're all familiar with the multitude of blogs that appear on the internet, but you may not understand exactly how bloggers make income from their blogs. With this chapter, I will provide some tips on how you can start a successful blog that can provide you with additional income. Like most passive income streams, starting a blog will require some time and effort. But once you are set up, your blogs can continue to provide income for months, weeks, and even years.

The Truth About Earning Through Blogs

I'm sure you're aware that there are millions of blogs on the internet. Anyone who has used Google or Bing can attest to the fact that there is a blog on the internet for just about every topic imaginable. Some of those blogs make money; some of them don't. Some of those blogs are intended to make money; others are not. Some of the blogs intended to make money do not make money. With this chapter, we will concentrate on blogs that are intended to make money and I will give you some tips and techniques as to how to create a blog and then how to monetize that blog.

Determine a Niche. In starting a blog that is going to provide you with additional income, you will first have to find a niche for that blog. A niche is a particular market segment or audience. Unless your blog has a specific niche or target audience, it's going to be very difficult for you to monetize it. Yes, there are bloggers on the internet who write about random topics or about anything and everything. But most of those bloggers don't make money from their blogs. Bloggers who make money from their blogs usually have specific topics or niches that they use to attract visitors to their site or solve specific problems.

In determining a niche for your blog, you should remember that most people visit blogs to gather information or to solve a specific problem. If you can provide them with the information they are looking for in an attractive package, then you'll have a chance to have a successful blog. It's important to note that whatever niche you choose, there are probably already existing blogs that already fall within that niche. Don't let this discourage you. If you can convey valuable information and you can convey it in a straightforward, entertaining, and attractive manner, you'll have a chance to be successful with your blog.

Here are examples of some of the most popular blog niches:

--How to Make Money.

--Health & Fitness.

--Lifestyle.

--Food.

--Personal Finance.

--Beauty and Fashion.

In choosing a niche for your blog, I strongly suggest that you select a topic or an area that you are passionate about. If you are passionate about something, you'll be much more likely to be able to write blogs about that subject. Your readers will be able to sense your passion and you'll be a lot less likely to abandon your blog or blog series because you've become bored with it or lost interest in it.

I'll give you an example. I have a close friend who is an avid baseball fan. His favorite team is the Minnesota Twins professional baseball team. My friend, who when I first met him was working a regular day job, is such a baseball fan that he spends almost all of his spare time thinking and talking about baseball. He lives and breathes baseball. One day, it dawned on him that he might be able to make money from his favorite hobby. So, he started a Minnesota Twins baseball blog in which he posted articles he wrote about his favorite team. He found quickly that there were many other Minnesota Twins fans who were desperate to read about their team every day and they wanted a daily dose of information about the Twins, even during the off-season. So, what started as a weekly blog, quickly became a daily blog or post. He now has a stable of regular contributors who contribute to his Minnesota Twins-themed website. He has a forum in which his site visitors or blog readers can comment on various subjects involving the Twins. The site now has semi-monthly podcasts in which he and some of his associates discuss the Twins. He is a guest on radio shows and talks about the Twins. Bottom line, he has turned his passion and his modest initial blogs into a full-time job. He is truly doing what he loves. His Twins website/blog spot now gets so many daily visitors that he is easily able to sell site advertising to companies that are looking to reach the same niche audience. Those advertisers include ticket brokers, bars and restaurants that are near the Twins stadium, travel agencies that coordinate spring training vacations to watch the Twins, etc. It's amazing to think that all of this started with one paltry blog and has blossomed into a full-scale profitable business.

In reviewing this example, it is important to remember that my friend selected a niche he was passionate about, one he was not going to lose interest in. He was going to think and talk baseball whether he had a blog or not. But in launching his blog, he quickly discovered that many people have the same passion he has, and he was able to monetize that passion into a profitable business.

If you want to determine a possible niche for your blog and you're not quite sure what a good niche would be for you, let me suggest that you ask yourself the following questions: What is your favorite hobby? How do you spend most of your free time? Is there a subject or topic that you could go on and on about if someone is willing to listen? What were your favorite subjects in high school or college? What things do you like to read about, learn about, or gather information on? If you were independently wealthy and you did not have to work for a living, what activities or pastimes would you choose to fill your time?

Write Some Blogs. Once you have determined your niche, you can start writing blogs. Instead of writing just one blog, I suggest that you write a series of blogs so you can post them on a regular basis (weekly, monthly, etc.). Prepare some kind of an outline in which you determine and detail the topics for each of your blogs. Some bloggers prefer to place all their content online at the same time and then leave it at that. For example, if the niche is targeted at bloggers and is How to Start and Make Money from a Blog, the blogger could post a number of blogs all at the same time. Topics for the individual blogs could include how to choose a blog niche, how to write a blog, how to choose a blog platform, ways to make money from your blog, etc. Each different topic could have a separate blog and, in reality, you could post all of these blogs at the same time and be done with the writing. On the other hand, if your niche requires or benefits from frequent updating, you'll want to write additional blogs as new information becomes available. For example, with the Minnesota Twins blog site I described, the Twins play 162 games in a regular season and it's reasonable to think that any blogs concerning the team will require at least weekly blogs. This particular site has become so successful that it now features new blogs on a daily basis. It's important to note that these blogs are not all written by the founder of the blog site. He now has a stable of writers who contribute blogs to the site on a regular basis.

What if you're not a writer? Can you still have a blog? Yes, you can. You can hire a freelancer to write your blogs. There are a number of freelancing sites you can use to hire a writer, including Upwork and Fiverr. If you want to convey specific information in your blogs, then you will obviously have to relay this information to the freelance writer. But I know other people who simply give the freelancer a topic and then the freelancer will research the topic and write the article. In hiring a freelancer, you should try to find someone that fits your style and someone you can work with on an on-going basis. You may have to go through a freelancer or two before you can find a freelancer that suits your needs. Depending on the length of your blogs, you should be able to find a freelancer that can write a blog for you at about $25 to $40 per blog. If research is required on the part of the freelancer, you can expect to pay more.

Select Your Platform. There are a lot of different platforms available for you to publish your blog. Some of them are free; others charge a nominal monthly fee to host your blogs. In this section, I'll detail a few of the options available to you and then you can research these options further as you decide which platform you should use.

1) **WordPress** is the most popular blogging platform. It is especially popular with beginner bloggers as it is free, it doesn't require a lot of technical expertise such as coding or design, and it has lots of different themes to choose from. Please know that WordPress

might not have the functionality you are looking for unless you pay for their upgrades. However, as a beginner, you can decide which "bells and whistles" you want to upgrade to later to make your site look more professional, to have access to more themes, designs, and plug-ins, etc. For example, WordPress.org charges about $3 a month for hosting and offers more than 1500 free themes and 20,000 free plug-in options. Again, if you are a beginner, I suggest that you start with the free package and see if that fits your needs. If not, you will be able to upgrade at any time.

2)   **Blogger** is a platform owned by Google. It's also free and offers free access to Google tools such as AdSense and Analytics. It is an easy platform to use and it's a great platform for beginner bloggers.

3)   **Tumblr** is another free platform that is a social media site. It's great for microbloggers, people who want to post many short notes frequently.

4)   **Typepad** and **WIX** are pay-per-month business platforms that charge nominal monthly hosting fees of less than $10 per month. Those platforms are geared toward business blogs. They are easy to use. WIX has ecommerce functions that make it attractive to small businesses. Unlike WordPress, Blogger, and Tumblr, both Typepad and Wix allow you to have your own domain name. For example, your domain name will always have wordpress (Wordpress) or blogspot (Blogger) in the title. This may not matter to you, but if you are a business, that might be an important consideration and you may want instead use a third party server such as BlueHost or HostGator to host

your site. Both of those third-party servers offer very reasonable pricing for hosting at less than $3 a month.

Promote Your Blog. Common sense tells us that no one is going to read your blog unless they know it exists. Some bloggers are reluctant to "toot their own horn" and tell others that they have a blog. Don't be shy about this. When you publish your first blog, use email blasts and social media to tell people you know about your new blog and tell them how they can access it. If you don't do this, then you may find that your mother is the only person reading it.

Use Your Blog to Expand Other Related Passive Income Activities. If you're smart, you will tie your blogs into your other passive income activities. Not only will this help produce additional income, it should also help you create a loyal following. Many people use their blogs to promote their newsletters. They will instruct readers to sign up for monthly or quarterly newsletters. Along the same lines, bloggers will direct their readers to the podcasts or the videos they have produced. I know quite a number of bloggers who have accumulated the blogs they've written over the years and compiled those blogs into eBooks. It's all interrelated. You should plan to have multiple venues to promote your passive income activities.

Seven Ways to Earn Income from Blogging

There are multiple ways you can make money from blogging. No, it's not an overnight process and there is some initial work required. However, once you're up and running, you could be able to supplement your income substantially by blogging. I've selected seven of my favorite ways for you to make money blogging. Here they are:

1) Cost-per-click (CPC) advertising. With this concept, advertisers will pay each time a visitor to your site clicks on one of the ads on your site. It's a "finder's fee" of sorts. CPC advertising can include full-color ads which appear on your site; it can also include simple text advertising in your blog. For example, if you have a baseball blog in which the topic is "Different ways to get tickets to the big game" and one of the options is to buy tickets from an authorized ticket broker, you would be able to mention the name of that ticket broker in your text, and, provided that the ticket broker is a participating advertiser, you'll be able to earn a small sum every time someone clicks on that ad and the ad takes them to the advertiser's site. I should mention up front that you're not going to get rich from CPC advertising until the numbers of people visiting your site reach respectable numbers. Companies that offer easy to implement CPC internet advertising include Google's AdSense, infolinks, media.net, and Chitika. If you have further interest in CPC advertising, I suggest that you visit some of these aforementioned sites to learn more about what advertising programs are available to you as a blogger.

2) Sell your own advertising on your blog. If you want, you can take it upon yourself to go "old school" and sell ads on your site. You can arrange yourself for advertisers on your site or you can have a third-party seller do that for you. To give you an example of a sell-your-own advertising approach, if you have a blog regarding a specific bike trail, you could certainly approach a bike rental place along that trail or a restaurant at one of the stops along the trail and see if they want to advertise on your blog. Nothing wrong with selling ads to your blog the old-fashioned way…and you will be able to keep 100% of the ad revenue yourself. If you don't want to bother with selling ads on your site, you can register with a third-party seller and they can do that for you. Companies like BuySellAds or BlogAds are third-party advertising sellers who will sell ads for your blog. They'll then give you 70 to 75% of the ad sales and then keep the remaining amounts in return for their efforts. Please note that third-party sellers are not interested in low-traffic blogs, so you'll have to get your traffic to a decent level before you can even consider using a third-party seller.

3) **Sell text links on your blog.** I mentioned text link advertising in the above section on CPC advertising. There is a company called LinkWorth that specializes in this kind of text advertising. With LinkWorth, you'll be able to link a piece of text in your blog to a page on another site. Every time one of your blog readers clicks on this link, you'll receive a commission from Linkworth. This is another program that requires a decent amount of traffic to your blog before you can begin working with LinkWorth, so if you're a new blogger and your blog traffic is still minimal, you'll have to get your traffic up before you can begin doing these cost-per-click text links.

4) **Online courses and workshops.** In the previous chapter, I told you how you could make money by self-publishing online courses and workshops. Any blog you do should link to any related online courses and workshops that you've produced. Again, all of these things are interrelated and you should never miss an opportunity to advertise one medium on another medium.

5) **Books and eBooks.** Just as you'll want to use your blog to promote your online courses and workshops, you'll want to use it to promote any printed books, digital books, or audiobooks which you have produced.

6)   Speaking gigs. Once your blog traffic has reached a reputable level, you will be able to advertise yourself as an expert on whatever subject your blog covers. This may bring speaking opportunities in which you can enhance your passive income. I had a recent speaking engagement which resulted from my blogs concerning the history of the small town I was born in. My audience was the town historical society and, although I didn't get paid for my speaking engagement, I was able to sell 71 of my printed books after my presentation. The presentation was well worth my time financially, as I made over $10 per printed book for a 90-minute presentation which I enjoyed immensely. So, if you're not yet someone who can command a fee of $10,000 to $100,000 per speech, don't worry about it. You can still achieve profits on a lower scale by using your blog to promote your products and services.

7)   Affiliate marketing. Affiliate marketing involves recommending or referring the products and services of other companies and their products and services in return for a commission. Are you recommending other products or services on your blog? Or could you recommend other products or services on your blog? If you do or if you can, then I suggest that you consider affiliate marketing to earn some passive income. Again, the money you can earn will be directly related to the number of people who read your blogs, however when your blog traffic reaches a respectable level, then it's time for you to start exploring affiliate marketing opportunities. There are a ton of affiliate programs available to you. I've listed some of the most popular programs for you to use as a starting point when your blog is at a level where you can start to reap the benefits of affiliate marketing. (I've provided additional information about affiliate marketing in the chapter that follows.)

--Amazon Associates

Passive Income Ideas

--eBay Partner Network

--BlueHost

--HostGator

--HostPapa

--DreamHost

--AliExpress

As I've detailed in this chapter, you will be able to earn passive income from your blog. Obviously, before you can do that, you'll have to get your blog up and running and get the traffic levels for that blog to a point where you can earn some extra cash from it. But once you've done that, you can start reaping the benefits from it.

Chapter 4—Make Passive Income on the Internet Now

Most of us have heard the term "make money while you are sleeping". Affiliate marketing is the passive income activity which is most often associated with the concept of making money while you are sleeping. In this chapter, I'll outline how you can make money with affiliate marketing and with dropshipping, another passive income activity which is often related to affiliate marketing. I'll tell you why you need to consider these activities for your passive income streams and I'll tell you how to get started.

All You Need to Know About Affiliate Marketing

Affiliate marketing is when you recommend or refer the products or services of other companies in return for a commission. With affiliate marketing, you are the affiliate. You search for products that you enjoy or would like to endorse and then promote that product through your various media, including websites, social media, written blogs or video blogs, and emails, and then you earn a portion of the profit when a sale is made for that product or service. Sales are tracked through affiliate links from one website to another.

I'll give you a quick example. A woman has a series of blogs or podcasts that are targeted at new parents. As a new parent herself, she has used a baby stroller which she really likes and would recommend to anyone. With these in mind, she writes one of her blogs or does one of her vlogs (video blogs) with this stroller brand as the main subject. She highly recommends the stroller based on her experience in using it and in her blog or vlog she provides a link to the site of the manufacturer, where customers can visit and subsequently purchase the stroller. For each stroller sold as a result of the woman's blog or vlog, the woman will receive a commission for her part in recommending the stroller and then telling the customer where they can purchase it.

As this book is being written, current statistics show that 81% of all brands and 84% of all companies are using affiliate marketing as a means to sell their products or services. Those percentages will continue to increase as companies continue to increase their affiliate marketing spending. In 2018, 16% of all internet sales resulted from affiliate marketing. That's an impressive number. Data now shows that companies selling products and services through affiliate marketing will spend 62% of what they would spend through traditional marketing efforts, so as these companies realize that they can spend less and be more successful in selling through affiliate marketing, they will begin to focus more of their sales efforts on that activity and affiliate marketing will continue to grow in future years.

From the consumer standpoint, consumers may or may not be aware that you will be earning a commission as a result of recommending a product or service. Either way, most of them won't care, as they will almost always end up paying the same price for the product. Your commission will be built into the retail price of the product and the consumer will not pay additional to cover your commissions.

As an affiliate, you can be paid for three different actions which direct the consumer to the seller. The most popular action will be Pay Per Sales. With this action, you direct the consumer to the seller and the consumer purchases the product. You can also get paid with a Pay for Lead action. Again, you direct the consumer to a seller site and the consumer then does any of a number of required actions, possibly completing a contact form, signing up for a product trial, subscribing to a newsletter, downloading software, etc. In these instances, the seller will value these actions enough to pay you a commission. Another form of affiliate marketing involves the affiliate being paid on a Pay Per Click basis. Usually, Pay Per Click involves the consumer clicking a link on your site to move to the seller's site. The seller values this enough to allocate a commission to the affiliate.

Why be an affiliate marketer? With affiliate marketing, you really can earn money while you are sleeping. Once you've invested an initial amount of time in promoting a product, you can continue to earn money for your efforts long after you recommended the seller's product or service. Once you have directed the consumer to the seller, you can step out of the transaction and don't have to spend any time in supporting the customer after the sale. Affiliate marketing is attractive to many people because it allows them to earn passive income from home without much initial investment and without having to create the product or service you're going to help sell. There are no affiliate fees to worry about and you can get started quickly without a lot of time or effort.

Five Steps Toward Becoming an Affiliate Marketer

How can you get started on your journey to becoming an affiliate marketer? Here are some simple steps you can take to become an affiliate marketer. By the time you complete these steps, you should be well on the road to becoming a successful affiliate marketer and earning passive income while you sleep.

1) **Find or determine a niche.** If you're going to get into affiliate marketing, you're going to have to determine a niche for that marketing. In determining a niche or niches for your affiliate

marketing, I strongly suggest that you find niches or areas that you are passionate about or strongly interested in.

I'll use myself and my wife as examples. In doing a personal inventory, I have a number of passions, many of which are my hobbies. I love baseball, especially Major League Baseball. I also love being a youth baseball coach. I also love reading and writing. I consider myself to be an expert on writing, ghostwriting, self-publishing, and editing. Finally, I love biking and I love dogs. My wife, on the other hand, loves to talk about parenting issues. She is a midwife by trade and is very knowledgeable about midwifery. She is a fashionista and is extremely knowledgeable and passionate about handbags, as our credit card statements attest.

In looking at your interests, you should now try to determine whether there is enough depth there for you to present yourself as an expert on the subject. Is there enough depth in the subject that you could write 25, 50, or 100 blogs about it? For my purposes, I could write a blog about baseball every day. On the other hand, even though I enjoy biking, I would find it difficult to write 25 to 50 blogs about biking.

If you have enough depth in the niche you are considering, the next thing to consider is whether you can make money in recommending products or services in that niche. With the interests of my wife and I, a couple of things pop out at me. Regarding my love for dogs, I am well aware that pet products and supplies are a huge industry. Even a smaller industry such as bicycling has a lot of different products available, including bikes, helmets, gloves, bike bags, water bottles, and bottle holders, bike tire repair kits, etc. Obviously, there is a market for women's handbags, thanks to my wife. On the other hand, it's my feeling that there isn't as much money to be made in the youth coaching, as there aren't many products required to coach a youth baseball team. Yes, uniforms, bats, and balls may be required, but most coaches already have sources for those products. Yes, there may be some online coaching workshops which may be available to sell or some books along the same lines, but the amount of products in this niche seems to be somewhat limited compared to the products available in the dog niche or even in the smaller biking niche. So, in taking an inventory of the things you're passionate about, you should determine if there is money to be made within those niches. If there aren't any or that many products to sell within that niche, then it's not a good affiliate marketing niche. No products mean no sales.

2) Are there affiliate marketing programs available within your niche? After you've settled on a niche that you're interested in, it's time for you to find out what's out there in terms of product and services you can promote with your websites, blogs, vlogs, and emails. For example, if I decide that I want to get into an affiliate marketing program regarding puppy training, I'd want to find out what products are out there that are related to puppy training or dog training. On a slightly broader scale, what products are out there that are related to puppies in general.

You'll have to spend some time researching this. But because the products and services you find will be the source of your income for this affiliate marketing endeavor, the time you spend will be well worth it. When you find these products or services, you should make sure they are of good quality. If you are marketing items of poor quality, it will surely damage your reputation or credibility. Many affiliate marketers will test products or services before recommending them. Also, you should make sure that the products you're recommending to consumers are products that you want to be associated with. It might behoove you to read the posted product reviews of any products or services you are considering for your affiliate marketing efforts.

As you find affiliate marketing programs within your niche, you should see if there are similar sellers to you within the niche. If so, that's probably a good indication, as other affiliates would probably not be recommending those sellers if they are not making money from it.

3) Time to build a site. Now that you've done your research, it's time for you to create a vehicle in which you can disseminate information to consumers. It's time to build a website. Although there are many different web hosts out there, many beginners use WordPress because it is easy to use and it's free (although upgrades are available). Building a website is much, much easier than ever before and you won't need to be a coder or a designer. No technical knowledge required.

In building a website, you have to first purchase a domain, which will be the address for your website. GoDaddy and NameCheap are both very popular sources from which you can purchase a domain name. The last time I looked, you could purchase domain names from both these companies at under $15 per year. In selecting your domain name, you should know that it's possible that the domain name you want is already in existence and you may have to come up with some other options.

After you have a domain name, you will have to find a host for your website. Again, GoDaddy is a popular option, as are BlueHost and HostGator, companies I previously mentioned. All three of those companies have plans that start under $3 a month. If you purchase your domain name and your web hosting from different companies, you will need to link the two together. However, this is a very easy process that is outlined on the abovementioned sites.

Now that you have purchased a domain name and selected a host for your website, it's time for you to install your content management system. (e.g., WordPress or whatever content management system you have chosen.) In the process of doing this, you'll have the chance to select a theme to use for your website. While most content management systems offer a large selection of themes to choose from, you should select a theme that works well with whatever niche you have chosen.

4) Create content for your website. Now that you have your domain name, your web host, and your theme, you can begin creating content for your website. Whatever content you create should certainly be related to the niche you have chosen. Your content should be interesting enough, engaging enough, or informative enough to keep your web visitors coming back. Here are some basic ideas on popular ways to convey content on affiliate marketing sites:

Reviews. Many affiliates will provide reviews of the products or services they are trying to sell. If possible, you will have used the products you're reviewing. This should help you immensely in reviewing the product. If you haven't used the product, many consumers may be able to sense that you haven't done so.

Blogs. Affiliates often use blogs to promote the items they are trying to sell. Although the blog doesn't necessarily need to be all about the item you're trying to sell, it should at least mention that product or service within the article in the appropriate place. Many blogs will address problems, questions, and then hopefully provide solutions or recommendations on how those problems can be solved. In working your affiliate marketing, you'll obviously want to recommend your affiliate products as possible solutions to the problems.

In-text Content Links. I'm sure you've visited websites and read articles which have links within the text of those articles. If you click on those links, they'll take you to other websites where you can view additional content or purchase products or services. These are called in-text context links and they provide a very effective means of affiliate marketing. By using in-text links, you'll be able to earn money if people from your site go immediately to these other sites and purchase products.

Informational Products. Many websites will offer free informational products to build their mailing lists. If you can build a substantial mailing list, you will be much more successful in your affiliate marketing. Affiliates will also offer free newsletters or free eBooks to consumers who register their names and email addresses.

Banner ads. Many affiliates use banner ads on their websites to direct people to their affiliate sites. These banner ads can be very effective, though you wouldn't want to clutter your site with so many ads that your content gets lost. You might also lose your credibility as an expert.

5)   Market your site, build your audience. Now that you have your website up and running, it's important to let people know it exists. There are a number of ways you can build the audience for your website. In doing this, it is important for you to continue adding valuable content to your site, content that will keep people coming back to your site. If someone is going to visit your site once and then never visit again, you're very unlikely to be successful in your affiliate marketing efforts. Here are ways you can build your following:

Social media. You're probably already participating in various social media venues. It's important for you to use those venues to promote your new website. Social media such as Facebook, Instagram, Twitter, and Pinterest offer opportunities for you to get the word out about your new site.

Expertise. If you are an expert in something (i.e.—puppy training), you should make yourself available to do guest posts on other related high-traffic blogs. Offer to write blogs to be posted on these other sites in return for them mentioning or providing a link to your web address. Guest posting on someone else's established site, you'll be able to get the word out about your website.

Search Engine Optimization (SEO). SEO will also be important in directing people to your website. If you're not very familiar with SEO, I suggest that you take some time to read a few articles on SEO and what you can do to optimize your website in internet searches. If you don't have the time to do this, you might consider hiring an SEO marketing expert to do this for you.

Paid advertising. Another option you can use to drive people to your website is paid advertising. Social media sites generally offer affordable ads. Or you can buy banner ads on small niche sites that are related to your niche. GoogleAdWords might also be a good option for you, depending on your niche.

Make Money Dropshipping

Dropshipping is yet another way for you to make passive income. For those of you who are not exactly sure what dropshipping is, let me provide a description that may help. Dropshipping is a retail fulfillment method in which you will be able to sell the retail products of your choice on an online store which you create. The benefit of dropshipping for you is that you will not need to open a brick-and-mortar store with its large overhead and monthly lease and insurance costs. You won't have to hire and pay employees or do payroll taxes. You won't have to carry or stock any merchandise. All of that will be handled by a third party, a supplier who will store and warehouse the items you're selling and who will ship the items you sell directly to the consumer.

You'll be responsible for securing sales for the items you are selling. You will also be able to set prices on these items, but those prices will have to be comparable to what the market dictates or offered by competitors or companies selling the same merchandise. It should be pointed out that with dropshipping programs, the products you are selling are likely to be sold by other companies as well, so your pricing will probably need to remain competitive and you might find that your profit margins will be slim, depending on the item.

Let me take you through how this process works behind the scenes. Let's say that I have an online store that sells custom minor league baseball jerseys. All of these jerseys contain the logos and designs of different minor league baseball teams. A customer purchases a jersey from my website for $40 and pays me online for that jersey. I then forward the order to my supplier or wholesaler, who is selling the jersey to me for $28. The supplier then sends the order to the customer using a shipping label with my name on it. This "blind label" is used so the customer will recognize the shipper of the item. It is also used so the customer will not be able to bypass me and go directly to the supplier or wholesaler. When the supplier or wholesaler ships the jersey to the customer, they will charge me for the $32 cost of the jersey plus shipping. So, my role in the entire sale is simple: I secured the sale and sent it to the supplier, and I sent an acknowledgment to the customer. The supplier made, stored, and shipped the jersey. I also collected a cool $8 for the sale. All in all, as an affiliate marketer, I am a middleman. As you can see, dropshipping is a simple business model that requires a minimal investment in time and money on your part. If you find the right niche and the right supplier, dropshipping can be a profitable venture.

Five Essential Steps in Creating Dropshipping Business

Here are five essential steps for achieving dropshipping success.

1) Find a niche. We've discussed how important it is to find a niche in the previous sections on blogging and affiliate marketing. The same principles apply here. If you're going to get involved in dropshipping, you'll be involved in a venue in which you're likely to have many competitors. With this in mind, the more you are able to refine your niche, the more successful you'll be. For example, if you want to fine-tune your niche, you can go from pet products down to dog products down to puppy products or dog training products, etc. You get the picture. The more you fine-tune your niche, the fewer your competitors and the higher your profit margins will be.

2) Research your competition. Speaking of competition, it will be important for you to research your competition to find out how much they are charging for the same or similar items you intend to sell on your site. This should give you an idea of the profit margins that will be involved with the items you're intending to sell. If you discover that you'll have to sell for low margins on most of the items you intend to sell, you might want to rethink the niche you have chosen.

3) **Select a platform.** With your dropshipping business, you'll have plenty of platforms to choose from. I'll outline three of the most popular platforms here to give you a good idea of what is available to you.

Doba has a huge selection of products and suppliers for you to use in your dropshipping activities. They have over 2 million products to choose from. These products come from nearly 200 suppliers. In working with Doba, you will not have to partner with multiple dropshippers. Doba charges $29 a month for its basic program and a 99 cents per order fee. They have live training webinars for newbies and they'll send you email updates regarding supplier discounts, new products and seasonal products, and new suppliers as they become available to you.

Oberlo is a platform which is tightly integrated with Shopify. It allows for easy one-click import of AliExpress products. Please know that Oberlo works only with Shopify stores and it only supports AliExpress for now. They offer a free account, but with the free account, you will be limited to 500 products and 50 orders per month. When your orders exceed 50 orders a month, your monthly fee will go to $29.90.

Dropship Direct has over 100,000 items from more than 900 brands for you to choose from. It's free to use, but as you grow your business, you'll note that they have a back-end management system that is available for $37/month or free to those who are doing over $1000 a month in sales.

Other dropship platforms that might merit a look include **Wholesale2B, Megagoods, SaleHoo, Sunrise Wholesale, Wholesale Central, and National Dropshipper.**

4) Build your ecommerce site. After you've determined which platform you're going to use for your dropshipping activities, you'll need to develop a website or a store on which to sell the products you've chosen. Most dropshipping newbies use Shopify for their ecommerce store. Shopify has a web-based site builder that will allow you to get your dropshipping business up and running quickly. You won't need a tech background to launch a website on Shopify. And with a Shopify site, you'll have complete control over your site's navigation, content pages, and design. Also, Shopify has a built-in payment processing system that will allow you to accept payments from customers who are purchasing items on your site. And Shopify has multiple apps which will help you in developing a successful dropshipping business. Additionally, Shopify has a number of pricing plans for you to choose from. Those plans start at $29/month and Shopify will take 2.9% of sales and 30 cents per transaction on top of the monthly fee.

5) Drive people to your site. Once you have your ecommerce site up and running, your work isn't finished. You're going to have to continue to work to get people to visit your site. You'll do this on social media, in your blogs and vlogs, and with emails. I have outlined most of these marketing activities in the chapter on affiliate marketing, so I won't repeat them here. But I do emphasize the importance of making people aware of your site, not just once, but on a continual basis. If you have good products to sell at reasonable prices, the key to growing your business will revolve around your ability to get people to visit that site.

Chapter 5—Get Richer While You Sleep

In this chapter, I'm going to show you some additional passive income streams to help you earn even more money while you sleep. Maybe you can even get to a point where you'll be making so much money while you sleep that you'll want to sleep all the time. Just kidding. (joke)

Amazon FBA

Amazon FBA stands for Fulfillment By Amazon. Amazon FBA has become one of the most popular ways to earn income online. There are almost 2 million people selling on Amazon worldwide. About half of the sales on Amazon come from third-party selling; of the top 10,000 Amazon sellers, about two-thirds of those sellers use FBA.

Here's how it works. You send your products to Amazon. They stock them and store them for you. When a customer orders one of your products, Amazon then picks, packs, ships, and tracks that product for you. They also handle all returns and refunds. Amazon then pays you every two weeks for any of the merchandise you have sold. In return for their efforts, Amazon charges storage fees and fulfillment fees.

There are a number of major advantages to using Amazon FBA to sell your items. Most importantly, they offer you immediate access to millions of potential customers. Over 300 million people have purchased from Amazon; they have over 90 million Amazon Prime members. Bottom line, no other company can even come close to offering you access to this many customers. And because of all the packages it ships and all the warehouses it has in different parts of the country, Amazon is able to ship and deliver items less expensively than anyone else. One of the biggest reasons people use Amazon is because of the free shipping they offer to their Prime customers and also to their non-Prime customers who place orders that achieve a minimum dollar amount. Also, Amazon is well-known for its prompt shipping, its great customer service, and its generous return policy. All of these things have allowed Amazon to build its reputation as a retailer, and the volume that Amazon generates shows the confidence that consumers have in the company.

If you're going to use Amazon FBA, you should be aware of the various fees associated with it. If you're just getting started, Amazon has an individual plan for those people who sell less than 40 items per month. There is no subscription fee for this plan. (Item-selling fees obviously still apply.) If you're selling more than 40 items a month on Amazon, the next step up is their professional selling plan, which has a monthly subscription charge of $39.99. (Again, item selling fees apply.) Individual plan sellers on Amazon pay a fee of .99 per item sold and variable closing fees of .45 to $1.35 per item. Professional sellers pay variable closing fees and referral fees ranging from 6% to 25%, averaging 13%.

If you're going to participate in Amazon's FBA program, you'll pay storage fees for Amazon to store your items in its warehouse. There are short-term and long-term storage fees. Short-term fees are monthly fees that vary depending on the time of the year the items are stored. From January through September, you have to pay about .65 per cubic foot; during the holiday season, October through December, you have to pay $2.40 per cubic foot. In addition to that, you'll need to pay long-term storage fees for any of your items which Amazon stores for over a year. Amazon takes what they call an inventory cleanup every February 15 and August 15 and they'll then notify you of any items you've had in their inventory for over a year. But you can avoid long-term storage fees if you submit a removal order and get those items out of the Amazon warehouse. Thus long-term storage fees should not be a major concern. Either way, it will also behoove you to stay on top of your inventory so you can minimize monthly storage fees and eliminate the possibility of any long-term fees.

In reviewing Amazon FBA success stories, I've noted that the biggest success stories involve sellers who are selling unique products or product niches. If you want to get rich selling through Amazon FBA, you'll want to have an extremely unique product, possibly even an item or concept that you have created. For example, Amazon FBA success stories include a man who created a toy card game and another man who created a concept on flipping used books for a profit. Still another man took an old concept that had lost steam and marketed it to a new audience. He took a pop-up basketball hoop and net that had previously sold in arcades, fairs, and bars, and remarketed it so it was targeted for home use. Someone else worked with a Chinese manufacturer to develop a line of ultra-comfortable shoes, while another scouted and made available a line of health products for pet lovers. And yet another selected trendy items that he could privately label and made them available. As you can see, most of these success stories involve unique products or concepts. If you have an item like this or if you can find one, you could have tremendous success on Amazon FBA.

All You Need to Know About Peer-to-Peer Lending Opportunities

Peer-to-peer (P2P) lending is another way you can make passive income, by using your money to make more money. For those of you unfamiliar with peer-to-peer lending, let me describe it to you. With P2P lending, individuals loan their money to individuals or small businesses that are looking to borrow money. In essence, P2P is non-bank lending which cuts out the middleman—the banks. P2P lending has become attractive to yield-seeking investors who are looking for alternatives to replace lower yield traditional investments such as savings, bonds, money market funds, and certificates of deposit.

If you're saying that you don't have money to invest, I should point out quickly that you won't have to invest large amounts. Many popular P2P lending companies, including Prosper and Lending Club, require a minimum investment of only $25 in each loan. Peer-to-peer lending generally offers a rate of return that ranges from 5 to 11%. P2P lending is generally considered safe, but, as with any lending, there is some risk involved, as the loans offered are unsecured loans.

Here's how P2P lending works. A person (or business) looking to borrow money goes to a P2P lending site and fills out an application that includes the reason they want to borrow money and the amount they are looking for. P2P loans range from $1000 to $35,000. That information is then made available to prospective investors who can choose what loans they invest in. Loans are priced and categorized based on numerous factors, including the prospective borrower's credit score, current income level, the requested loan amount, and the desired term of the loan. It's important to note that almost all lending platforms do not entertain sub-prime borrowers. In fact, most of the lending platforms require a minimum credit score of 600 to 650 and they typically don't make loans to people or businesses that have had recent bankruptcies, judgments, or tax liens.

With P2P lending, the platform handles all of the administrative tasks involved in the loans, including underwriting, closing, distribution of the loan, and collection of the monthly payments. In return for that, the lending platforms take a management fee (usually 1%) for their role in administrating the loan. This management fee is subtracted from each monthly payment. With P2P lending, all the investor has to do is to select the loans they want to invest in.

As mentioned above, there is some risk in investing in P2P loans. The main risk is the possibility of default. As these are unsecured loans, you could stand to lose the money you've invested if the borrower defaults on the loan. And there is no FDIC insurance on these loans. So, worst-case scenario, the money you invest in P2P lending could decrease instead of increase. Another thing to remember is that these investments have limited liquidity. So, once you've invested, you probably won't be able to get your money out until the term of the loan has expired.

In going into the details of the possible risks of P2P lending investment, I don't do so to discourage you from participating in this form of investment. I just want you to beware of the possible pitfalls which are associated with P2P lending. Most lending platforms will rank the risk involved with each loan and some of the platforms allow you to invest in all of their different risk categories. This allows the investor to diversify his portfolio and the offset higher risks with lower risks.

I've listed some of the most popular lending platforms for investors with a brief description for each:

Prosper is one of the most popular P2P lending platforms. It allows investors to invest a minimum of $25 in a loan. Prosper has seven different risk categories that have estimated returns ranging from about 5% to 13-1/2%. It allows investors to spread their risks out over all categories so they can diversify their portfolios and balance their overall risks.

Lending Tree is another popular site. With Lending Tree, you can invest as little as $25 in any loan, but you'll still need to transfer a minimum of $1000 into your account. With this platform, if you don't want to select loans manually, they'll let you choose a platform mix or a custom mix.

Peerform has 16 different risk categories. They allow investors to invest in whole loans or fractional loans. Also, they'll allow you to spread your loans over the different risk categories, so you can diversify your portfolio and average out your risks at a level you're comfortable with.

Here are some other popular platforms you might be interested in: Upstart, StreetShares, FoundingCircle, and Kiva. StreetShares and FundingCircle target small business loans. Kiva targets loans for non-profit organizations.

40 Ways You Can Use Your Skills or Interests to Earn Passive Income

This will be fun. In rapid-fire fashion, I'm going to throw out some quick ideas on how you might use your skills or interests to earn passive income. I won't spend a lot of time or space on these ideas, as that would take an entire book itself. However, I'm hoping that at least some of these ideas will be helpful to you. I offer a wide range of ideas and I'm offering them randomly. You'll realize immediately that some of the ideas are not for you, but hopefully some of them will spark some interest for you.

Passive Income Ideas

1) **Take Online Surveys.** You can make money in your spare time by completing surveys online. There are lots of online research firms that will pay you to complete surveys. Start with **Survey Junkie** and then if you still have extra time, register with other companies.

2) **Freelance Writer.** Are you a writer? If so, you can make extra cash by writing articles, blogs, books, web copy, etc. Start with **Upwork** and **Contently**.

3) **Freelance Editor.** Are you good at editing? If so, you can make money editing blogs, thesis papers, articles, web copy, books, etc. Again, start with **Upwork** and **Contently**.

4) **Paint Houses.** Do you like painting? Are you good at it? If so, you should be able to make some extra cash painting houses, inside or out. Your client buys the paint, but you'll have to supply the other necessary materials.

5) **Sell Your College Class Notes.** If you take good notes, you can probably make some extra money by selling notes to students who are taking the same classes the following semester.

6) **Sell Your Plasma.** I did this when I was in college. Unlike blood, which can be donated only every eight weeks, you can sell your plasma up to twice a week, at $25 to $50 per session. If you have a plasma center near you, this is a great way to earn extra cash. Most cities now have plasma centers. If you are attending a large university, there is almost certainly a plasma center nearby.

7) **Sell Your Photographs.** Are you a good photographer? Do you like to take photos? Well, you can sell those photos to stock photo sites and you can sell the same photo again and again. Who buys these stock photos? People buy them to use on websites, in blogs and newsletters, on book covers, etc. It's expensive to hire a photographer, and many people prefer to instead purchase photos from a stock photo site. Start with **istockphoto, SmugMug Pro,** and **Shutterstock.**

8) **Make, Grow, Sell Things at Farmer's Markets.** Do you have a farmer's market in your community or a surrounding community? If so, these are great places to sell lots of homegrown or homemade items, including fruits and veggies, baked goods, crafts, quilts, and homemade honey, syrup, or salsa. Check out the nearby farmer's market and see if it offers you the possibility of selling any of your homegrown or homemade items.

9) **Sports Tutor.** Are you knowledgeable about sports? If so, you might consider being a sports tutor. If you are a good baseball player, you might consider offering your services to teach kids how to improve their hitting skills. Were you a quarterback in high school or college? Teach aspiring quarterbacks how to improve their throwing skills. Tennis? Soccer? Gymnastics? Many parents are willing to spend money to have their kids improve their sports skills.

10) **Math Tutor.** Along the same lines, if you're good at mathematics you can sell your services as a math tutor. I have a daughter that did that for middle school kids and she earned some nice part-time income tutoring kids in math.

11) **Second Language Tutor.** Again, along the same lines, if you are proficient at a second language, you can teach/tutor students to learn another language. And with all these tutoring ideas, you should note that you can do that tutoring in person or online, individually or in group sessions. A friend of mine has a son who is paying for his post-college trip across Europe by teaching English to Chinese students online.

12) **Voice-Over Work.** Do you have a good voice? If so, you can earn extra money doing freelance voice-over work. Start with **Upwork** or **Fiverr** to find your gigs.

13) **Get Paid to Shop.** Many people now use personal shoppers for a variety of reasons. Some people use personal shoppers to do their holiday gift shopping (I saw that in a Hallmark movie). My neighbor

lady is 92 years old and she pays a woman to do her weekly grocery shopping. Some corporate executives who don't have much time to spare will hire someone to run errands, such as picking up dry cleaning.

14) **Handyman Gigs.** Good handymen are hard to find. If you're good at fixing things around the house, you should consider hiring yourself out as a handyman. Start with **Angie's List, Takl,** or a classified ad in your local newspaper.

15) **Housecleaning.** You can earn extra cash by hiring yourself out as a housecleaner, either on a continual basis, such as once a week, or you can sell your services to people who are moving and may not have time to clean their places properly before leaving. Again, start with **Angie's List and Takl.**

16) **Housesitting.** Yes, some people will let you live in their homes for free if they are going to be gone for extended periods of time. No parties, please.

17) **Yard Work Services.** Some people are not interested, not able, or don't have the time to do their own yard work. You can fill the void by mowing the lawn, shoveling snow, cleaning gutters, raking leaves, trimming bushes, etc.

18) **Sewing Services.** Are you good with a sewing machine? Can you mend clothes or shorten a pair of trousers? If so, you can make extra money at home sewing. Also, please note that some people make extra cash ironing or pressing clothes from their homes.

19) **Babysitting.** A great way for a responsible high schooler or college student to earn some extra cash.

20) **Pet Sitting.** Along the same lines, many pet owners don't know what to do with their pets when they are going away and can't take their pets with them, as the rising popularity of pet hotels shows. If you're a pet lover, this is a good way to earn some extra income. Put the word out.

21) Dog Walking. Yes, some people don't have the time to walk their dogs. This offers you an opportunity to make some money and get some exercise at the same time.

22) Teach Exercise Classes. If you're an exercise buff, you can earn extra income teaching exercise classes such as spinning, yoga, Zumba, CrossFit, etc. Make money while staying in great shape.

23) Phone-A-Friend/Welfare Check. One of my neighbors started a company in which she does a daily welfare check on elderly persons. She has assembled a nice roster of clients and calls each person at the same time every day. Her services are mostly paid for by the daughters or sons of the elderly person who are concerned about the welfare of the elderly parent.

24) Crafts. Are you good or could you be good at a particular craft? If you handmake jewelry, leather goods, clothing, etc., you can sell your items on various crafts platforms. Start with **Etsy** as the place to sell your items.

25) Small Engine and Motor Repair. Are you good at fixing small engines? Lawnmowers, snowblowers, boat motors? If so, there's money to be made in doing so. Same goes for simple appliances such as washers, dryers, refrigerators, etc.

26) Photography. Are you good with a camera? If so, you might hire yourself out for special events such as weddings, anniversary celebrations, proms, family holiday card photos, family pet photos, etc.

27) Music Lessons, Musical Instrument Lessons. Are you a good vocalist? Good at the piano, the drums, the guitar? Earn extra cash by giving lessons to people trying to become better singers or musicians.

28) Dance Instructor. Are you a good enough dancer to be able to teach it? Are you good enough to offer lessons to a couple who wants to learn or refine their dancing before their wedding day?

29) Mystery Shopping. Many national retail companies have mystery shopping programs in which they will send an anonymous mystery shopper to see how their customers are being treated. You can get paid to visit restaurants and retail locations. Start with **Best Mark** or **Market Force** to see what mystery shopping opportunities are available in your area.

30) Window Cleaning. This is another job that people will pay other people to do. Window cleaning requires a minimal amount of tools.

31) Computer, Electronic Device Repair. Are you good at this? Many people are willing to pay a nice fee for someone to repair their computer or other electronic devices. A lot of times, these are very simple problems and the customer simply isn't tech-savvy.

32) Caricature Artist, Face Painter. My niece is very talented at drawing caricatures. She can sketch a caricature in about 10 minutes and would often take her easel and pencil to various major events around town and offer to do sketches, for a fee of course. She did that at major concerts and sporting events. Also, she went to the beach on days when a lot of people were there and offered to do caricature sketches. Along the same lines, she learned how to face paint and then used that skill to make extra money at college football games.

33) Design T-Shirts. Do you have a knack for coming up with designs for things like t-shirts, bumper stickers, coffee mugs, etc.? If so, check out CafePress. You can place your designs for sale on that site; and then, when customers order a t-shirt with one of your designs, you'll earn a portion of the profits. CafePress will ship the item to the customer and collect the money. You won't have to do a thing other than to load the design.

34) Private Cooking Lessons. Are you a great cook? If so, you can earn some extra cash by teaching other people how to cook. Maybe some people will just want to learn the basics of cooking. Others might want to learn how to make desserts or bake pies. Others might want a crash course in Italian cooking or French cooking. You get the picture. You can make extra money teaching others what you're already good at.

35) Organize Homes or Offices. Are you good at organizing things? You can help people get rid of the clutter in their homes and offices.

36) Website Design. Are you an expert at web design? If so, your skillset offers you a great opportunity to earn extra cash. And you can do it all on the internet. Looking to get some web design gigs? Start with **Upwork** and **Fiverr.**

37) Drive for Cash. Do you have a reliable car? Know how to get around in the city you live in? You can make money by driving people to their destination. Many of you have heard of **Uber** or **Lyft.** If you'd rather not drive people around, there is an on-demand delivery service called **Postmate** in which you will be paid to deliver groceries, restaurant meals, liquor store orders, etc.

38) Videographer. Have a video cam? Good at turning pictures into videos? Then you should be able to make cash as a videographer. Start with special events like wedding receptions, birthday parties, anniversaries, family and class reunions, etc.

39) Graphic Design Services. Most small businesses can't afford expensive ad agencies to design their various marketing materials. But if you are proficient at graphic design, you have the opportunity to earn extra cash as a designer. You should be able to find some design gigs on **99 Designs.**

40) Home Staging. Can you make a home look attractive, inviting, and welcoming? It's common knowledge that staged or decorated homes sell much faster and for more money than empty homes. If you enjoy doing this, contact your local real estate agencies to see if they would be interested in this service. You'll also have no problem in working for multiple agencies, as the homes will already be listed by a specific real estate agency by the time the house is staged.

Chapter 6--Make Killer Investments

In this chapter, I'll provide you with beginner's information on three other passive income revenue streams: stocks, CDs (certificates of deposit), and real estate. I'm detailing these passive income opportunities in the final chapter of the book, as, in most instances, these are "use money to make more money" opportunities. Although large amounts of money are not required for any of these activities, you'll need to at least have some money to start with to participate in these investment opportunities.

How to Start Investing in Stocks

If you've never invested in stocks, it's important for you to know that investing in stocks isn't as complicated as it might seem. There are now many easy to use tools available to help you invest in stocks, whether you want to take a hands-on or hands-off approach. If you're considering investing in stocks, one of the most important things to remember is that investing in stocks is a long-term game. It's not meant to be a get-rich-quick scheme. In other words, you shouldn't invest money in stocks that you might need in the short term. This includes any emergency funds you might have tucked away. The reason for this is that many stock investments will fluctuate and, if you need to get out of these investments because you need cash for other things, you'll be subject to wherever the market is at that time. And, if the market or your stocks are down, you may even lose money on your original investment. It's been proven that most stock investments will continue to increase in value over time, but the market will fluctuate and you'll want to make sure you're not in a position where you have to withdraw your funds when the market and your investments are tracking down. As a rule of thumb, you should be comfortable parting with your money for at least five years. Why five years? That's because history shows that even if the market takes a downturn, it's very unlikely that a downturn would last longer than five years.

If you've yet to invest in the stock market and you're wondering if you can invest even if you don't have much money, the answer is yes, although there are some challenges. These challenges can be overcome, but you need to be aware of them before you begin investing. The first challenge to overcome is that many stock investments require a minimum. The second challenge involves diversification. With stock investing strategies, it's common practice to diversify your investments so you will not have "all your eggs in one basket". If you have limited funds, it's going to be difficult to spread your limited funds around.

The solution to both of these challenges is to invest in stock index funds and ETFs (exchange-traded funds). For those of you not familiar with exchange-traded funds, you should know that ETFs are investment funds traded on the stock exchange, much like stocks. ETFs hold assets such as stocks, commodities, or bonds. While mutual funds might require a minimum investment of $1000 or more, stock index fund minimums tend to be lower and ETFs tend to be even lower than index funds. As a matter of fact, some brokers offer index funds with no minimum at all. (Fidelity and Charles Schwab are two of the brokers that offer index funds without minimums.) So, not only are index funds available without minimums, they also have a built-in solution to the diversification problem, as index funds consist of many different stocks within a single fund.

If you're interested in receiving a passive income stream for your stock investments without having to sell the stocks you've invested in, you might consider dividend stocks, stocks that pay dividends. Well-established companies such as Target, Pepsico, Exxon, or Disney are more likely to pay dividends than some of the newer and less-established companies. The more established companies no longer need to invest all of their profits into growing the company and they can afford to pay out profits to their investors. On the other hand, newer companies, especially tech or biotech companies, are a lot less likely to pay out dividends, as they want to use as much of their profit as possible to expand the company.

There are two main types of dividends—cash dividends and stock dividends. These dividends are often paid quarterly, although some are paid monthly or semi-annually. Dividends offer a way for companies to distribute revenue back to investors and one of the ways investors earn a return from investing in the stock. Cash dividends are paid per each share of stock that you own. For example, if you own 20 shares in a company's stock and that company pays $2 in annual dividends, you will receive $40 per year for your stock shares. Some companies pay stock dividends instead of cash dividends, so instead of getting cash from your investment, you'll receive additional company stock. You'll then be able to sell that stock if you wish to get cash or you'll be able to keep it invested in the company. Some companies offer dividend reinvestments programs, called DRIPs, in which investors are allowed to reinvest their dividends back into the company's stock, often at a discounted rate. So, if you are interested in receiving a passive income stream from your stock investments, you'll want to specifically choose dividend stocks for your portfolio.

Now that I've given you some basic information on stocks, you should be ready to start investing. Here are some simple steps to get you started:

Determine if you're going to be a hands-on or hands-off investor. If you want to be heavily involved in choosing the stocks you invest in, you're going to need a stockbroker. I'm going to recommend three different brokers that are well-suited for beginning investors:

1)   **Merrill Edge.** A good choice for beginning stock investors, as no minimum deposit is required. Charges $6.95 per trade.

2)   **TD Ameritrade.** Another good choice for beginners. Like Merrill Edge, no minimum deposit required and a $6.95 charge per trade. Currently running a promotion in which trade charges are waived for 60 days, but with a qualifying deposit. With any broker you're considering, please check their sites to see what promotions they are offering. These promotional offers are always subject to change, so what's offered one month might next be available the next month.

3)   **E-Trade** requires a minimum account balance of $500, but they also have a promotion offering a cash credit, up to $600, for a qualifying account deposit. $6.95 charge per trade.

If you don't want to be heavily involved in selecting the stocks you invest in, you should consider using a robo-advisor account instead of a stockbroker. Most major brokerages offer robo-advisors, as they are extremely cost-efficient for the casual investor. In using a robo-advisor, you can get all the benefits of stock investing without having to do all the research you would have to do if you selected the stocks that you wanted to invest in. Robo-advisor services cover complete investment management. When you go to register for a robo-advisor, you'll be asked a series of questions regarding your investment goals. From that information, the robo-advisor will build a portfolio that fits with your goals and objectives. Here are three different robo-advisors which are well-suited for beginning investors:

1) **Wealthfront.** $500 account minimum with a 0.25% management fee. Please note that the 0.25% management fee is substantially less than you would pay a human investment manager.

2) **Betterment.** No account minimum with a 0.25% management fee that can be free for up to a year with a qualifying deposit.

3) **SoFi.** $100 account minimum with 0% management fees.

One other note before we move on from stocks to CDs: One of the best stock investment options for beginners is mutual funds. Mutual funds offer an easy and low-cost way for you to get your feet wet in the stock market. An S & P 500 fund is a great place to start. For those of you that have heard the term S & P fund, but don't know what it means, an S & P fund is a fund consisting of stocks from the 500 largest US companies. If you invest in an S & P fund, you'll be purchasing a small slice of 500 of the country's most successful companies. As these companies are already proven entities, you'll be investing in a group of companies that is likely to continue to thrive.

In a similar vein, if you are using a robo-advisor, the advisor will be able to create a portfolio of stocks from successful companies with which you'll be able to own a sliver of each of these customers and diversify your portfolio. These are low-risk stock investments, as the companies you'll be invested in will be proven entities.

All About CD Laddering

Before we get into CD laddering, I'll define what a CD is. A CD is a certificate of deposit. It is a time deposit that is commonly sold by banks, credit unions, or thrift institutions. CDs offer a very low-risk alternative to people who are looking to get higher interest rates than the meager interest rates they get on their savings accounts. The trade-off is that with a savings account you can generally take out your money at any time without a withdrawal penalty. With a CD, you will not be able to access your money for the length of the deposit, whether it is a one-year deposit or a five-year deposit.

CD laddering is a very simple process. CD laddering involves purchasing multiple CDs at the same time, with each CD maturing at different times. e.g., 1-year, 3-year, 5-year. Instead of placing all of your CD money in the same time interval, you will choose different intervals. CD laddering offers total flexibility. You can purchase different amounts for different intervals; you can even choose different banks for your different CDs, depending on the interest rates offered by those different banks. For example, if you have $10,000 to invest in CDs, you could invest $3000 in a 1-year CD, $3000 in a 2-year CD, $2000 in a 3-year CD, and $2000 in a 5-year CD. Maybe you use one bank for the 1- and 2-year CDs and another bank for the 3- and 5-year CDs because they are offering a higher interest rate than the first bank is offering on those intervals.

CDs already guarantee a rate of return. By laddering, you can get even higher interest rates and you'll always be close to having money that is available for any unexpected emergencies.

Let me give you another example to show how you can earn additional interest by laddering your CDS. Again, let's say you have $10,000 to invest in CDs. If you invest all $10,000 in 1-year CDs and continue to roll those CDs over as they mature, on an annual percentage yield of 2.8%, you will have increased your $10,000 to $11,502.68 in a 10-year period. On the other hand, if you take that same $10,000, and invest $2000 each in 1-,2-,3-,4-, and 5-year CDs, you'll get the higher interest rates as the length of the term increases. If you are getting the 2.8% interest on a 1-year, 2.95% on a 2-year, 3% on a 3-year, 3.05% on a 4-year, and 3.15% on a 5-year, you original $10,000 will have increased to $11,668.36 after 10 years.

Four Simple Ways to Make Real Estate Investment Income

Investing in real estate offers lucrative opportunities for you to earn additional passive income. One of the exciting things about investing in real estate properties is that, unlike stocks and bonds, you can pay for just a portion of your real estate investment before you can begin making money from it. Normally, you'll pay 20 to 25% as a down payment for the real estate you purchase. In some instances, you might even pay as low as 5%. Regardless of what your percentage is, from the time you sign your mortgage papers, you'll be able to start earning money from that investment.

Let's look at four simple ways you can make money from your real estate investments:

1) **Become a landlord.** If you buy a house or a small commercial property, you'll be able to make money by renting out that property. The upside of this is obvious. You'll be able to use your renter's payments to pay your mortgage. In many instances, you will be charging your renters a monthly rent that is more than your monthly mortgage payments. So, not only can you make money on your monthly payments from a renter, you can also use them to make your mortgage payments and increase your equity in the property as the property is probably appreciating.

In all fairness, there are some possible negatives involved in being a landlord. Unless you pay a company to manage your property, you'll be stuck with handling any problems at that property. If the hot water heater goes out, you'll be responsible for replacing it as soon as possible. If the washing machine, stops working, you have to either get it fixed or replace it…in most instances, at your expense. If you rent to bad tenants, it's possible that they can damage or destroy your property. If they don't pay their monthly rent, you're still going to have to make your mortgage payment and you might even have to pay to evict those tenants. If you can't rent your property and it's vacant, you're still going to have to make the mortgage payment.

That said, if you ever get to a point where your mortgage is paid off, the rent you collect will become almost all profit. At the same time, as you own the property for a period of time, that property is probably going to appreciate and you'll have a much more valuable asset than you started with.

2) **Real estate investment groups** are a great option for people who want to own real estate but don't want the hassles of being a landlord or managing a property. In a typical real estate group, a company buys or builds a set of apartment buildings or a condominium complex. They then allow people to purchase the units within those building or complexes. A person who buys a unit then becomes part of the real estate investment group. A single investor can own one or multiple units in the buildings or complexes, but the company operating the investment group will continue to manage all units, handle all maintenance, advertise vacancies, and secure tenants, in

return for a certain percentage of the monthly rent. If you are in a real estate group and your particular unit has a vacancy, you'll still receive a monthly payment, as any vacancies will be covered by the entire investment group. As long as there are not a lot of vacancies in the building or complex, you should still be able to derive monthly income from the unit(s) you own.

3) **Real estate trading (flipping).** This is the wild side of real estate investing. Real estate trading is very risky, but it can also be extremely lucrative. Flipping is not for the "weak of heart". If you're going to be successful at flipping, you are most likely going to have to be good at evaluating real estate and then marketing that real estate. There are two types of flippers. The pure flipper is interested in buying properties that require very little or no alteration. They will simply want to resell the property for more than they paid for it. The other type of flipper buys reasonably priced properties with the idea of renovating them or improving them to a point where they can then be resold at a profit. This is often a longer process than pure flipping, but profits can be substantial. If you're going to do this type of flipping, you're going to have to be willing to secure contractors who can renovate the property and you're going to have to be willing to oversee this work. Some people get into flipping without an idea of who to hire or what it is going to cost to make the improvements they want to make to give the property more value. If you've been hooked on the TV shows that revolve around house flipping or if you've been reading some of the tremendous success stories regarding flipping, you should know there are also many stories out there concerning newbies who expected to make their fortunes by flipping homes, but got in over their heads and had a disastrous flipping experience

4) **Real estate investment trusts (REITs)** are basically a more formalized version of real estate investment groups. A REIT is created when a corporation (or trust) uses investor money to buy and operate income properties. Unlike the aforementioned real estate investment groups, REITS include non-residential properties or real estate ventures, such as shopping centers, malls, and office complexes. REITs are bought and sold on the major exchanges, just like stock. With REITs, a corporation must pay out 90% of its excess profits to investors as dividends in order to maintain its REIT status. In doing this, REITs do not have to pay corporate income taxes, whereas a regular company would be taxed on its profits and then have to decide whether or not to issue dividends to investors from its after-tax profits. REITs are considered to be a solid investment for investors who want regular income.

Conclusion

Is there a better time than now to start earning more money? With all the passive income streams I've provided you in this book, you can no longer say that you don't have any ideas as to how you can earn some extra money. No one would ever pretend that all of these ideas will suit you, however there are definitely some ideas that you can pursue. Now the question is, are you going to spend your time complaining that you don't have any extra income streams or are you going to do something about it? I've given you the tools to be successful. What you do with those tools is up to you. When you were a kid and got a brand-new toy for your birthday, did you wait to use that new toy? I'll guess that you started playing with that new toy immediately. The same goes for the ideas in this book. Surely, you found at least a few good ideas among all the options I presented. Excuse the analogy, but now that you've read this book, the bus has just dropped you off at the road to success. Are you going to get on that road or are you going to get back on the bus?

Whether you use your money to make more money or whether you simply use your skills to make money, it's time to start now. I doubt that you would have read this book if you were not interested in making more money. Yes, most of the ideas presented will require some time or effort on your part. However, if you are willing to put in the initial effort, many of the ideas presented will allow you to earn extra money, some of it while you sleep. Checking your bank account balance can become something you look forward to instead of something you'd rather not do at all.

Whether you embark on micro-investing, blogging, peer-to-peer lending, or just walking dogs, there's no better time than now for you to start earning more money.

Financial Freedom Investing

Table of Contents

INTRODUCTION 102

CHAPTER 1: THE BUILDING BLOCKS OF FINANCIAL FREEDOM 106
IMPORTANT MINDSET SHIFTS TO START ACCRUING WEALTH 106
ESSENTIAL STEPS FOR ACHIEVING FINANCIAL FREEDOM 107
HOW TO SET YOUR FINANCIAL GOALS 111
SETTING YOUR SHORT-TERM AND LONG-TERM GOALS 115
10 WAYS TO GET OUT OF DEBT ASAP 116

CHAPTER 2: HOW TO BUDGET THE RIGHT WAY 122
HOW TO FIND A BUDGET THAT WORKS FOR YOU 122
6 MUST-KNOW BUDGETING METHODS TO NEVER LOSE TRACK OF MONEY AGAIN 124
WHICH BUDGET IS RIGHT FOR YOU? 129
7 WAYS TO MAKE BUDGETING MORE ENJOYABLE 130
7 IMPORTANT STEPS FOR BUILDING GOOD CREDIT 134

CHAPTER 3: INVESTING 101 139
TYPES OF INVESTMENTS TO ADD TO YOUR PORTFOLIO 139
TIPS ON CHOOSING THE RIGHT STOCKS FOR YOU 148
WHAT IS AN INVESTMENT PLAN? 151
THE 5 BEST STOCK TRADING STRATEGIES OF ALL TIME 153
8 WORST INVESTING MISTAKES TO AVOID 154

CHAPTER 4: DIVIDEND STOCKS 158
WHEN A COMPANY PAYS DIVIDENDS 158

DIFFERENT TYPES OF DIVIDENDS 159
CHOOSING STOCKS THAT PAY HIGH DIVIDENDS 163
HOW TO FIND THE BEST DIVIDEND STOCKS FOR YOUR PORTFOLIO 165
DO NOT MAKE THESE 10 DIVIDEND INVESTING MISTAKES 166
WHAT YOU NEED TO KNOW ABOUT DIVIDEND TAX RATES............ 169
ORDINARY VS. QUALIFIED DIVIDENDS 170

CHAPTER 5: DAY TRADING 172

WHAT IS DAY TRADING? 172
HOW TO START DAY TRADING 173
DAY TRADING STRATEGIES 177

CHAPTER 6: REAL ESTATE INVESTING 183

INCREASING YOUR PROPERTY VALUE 183
MAKING MONEY FROM RENTAL PROPERTY 184
HOW TO SELECT A TARGET MARKET 191
10 IMPORTANT FEATURES OF PROFITABLE REAL ESTATE 197
TOP 15 REAL ESTATE INVESTING STRATEGIES 200

CHAPTER 7: OTHER WAYS TO GROW WEALTH 203

HOW TO START INVESTING IN EXCHANGE-TRADED FUNDS (ETFS). 203
START MAKING MONEY NOW WITH PEER-TO-PEER LENDING 207
THE 10 BEST STRATEGIES FOR TRADING CRYPTOCURRENCIES 209
7 MUST-HAVE APPS FOR MODERN-DAY INVESTORS 213

CONCLUSION 217

Introduction

All of us seek financial freedom for different reasons. It could be that you want this freedom so that you can secure enough money to live comfortably in your retirement years. Others may be looking to purchase a new home, and still others may be planning a nest egg for their later years.

Planning how you will support yourself in your retirement can be stressful, and most people have money concerns looming over their heads. How many times have you turned on the news only to hear that some wealthy individual has just filed for bankruptcy? You might be wondering, *If he can't manage it with all his money, then what chance do I have?*

It is a legitimate concern. A look back through our recent history tells us that times have changed. We can no longer rely on job security to carry us through our lives. Jobs that you could stay on for 30 years or more and retire on a handsome pension plan are now few and far between. If we want financial freedom in this modern world, we need to learn how to think differently.

The challenge that we all face is how to get that financial security without relying on the traditional methods past generations took for granted. Those days are over, and we all need to plan our financial future more creatively.

In such situations, it can be difficult to know where to start. Maybe you're thinking about investing, but you don't know enough about it to make wise decisions. You're afraid of losing your hard-earned money on a high-risk gamble. Or maybe you're just tired of living paycheck to paycheck and you see that you need to think differently.

Or you're getting older and your body doesn't want to work as hard as it has before. Whether you're getting up in years and planning for retirement or you're just starting out and you're saving for a big purchase or investment, it makes sense that you start here with us.

There are many ways that we can meet this challenge. We have all learned how difficult it is to just put your money in a savings account and wait for it to grow. The interest rates they offer is such a pittance that you probably feel like you're actually paying the bank to hold your money rather than making anything off of it.

If you've thought about any of these things before, then you've come to the right place. You will be joining many others of like minds who have the same questions. In the following pages, we will show you how you can achieve a level of financial wealth that will put you on a sure footing, where you won't have to worry about your finances. Here, you will find:

- A beginner-friendly guide to investing and various investment options
- Ideas for how to make more money without much extra work needed
- Tips on making both short- and long-term goals and why they are important
- Essential information that can apply to a wide variety of financial needs.

There are plenty of alternatives to growing your cash and setting up a secure future for yourself. The answers are out there for anyone who has the wherewithal to look. They are not new, magical, or even mystical. This book is designed specifically to teach you some of those alternatives and how utilizing them can make a huge difference in helping you to achieve your financial freedom.

We've been taught that the fastest way to any destination is in a straight line. Unlike savings, however, this is not always the case. Investing requires that you take a few turns here or there and you may very well hit a few bumps in the road along the way. But, if you stay the course, your investment decisions could easily help you achieve financial freedom much sooner than you might think.

Once you apply the principles in this book, the rewards for your hard work will definitely be worth it. You will have:

- Freedom from money worries
- Freedom from debt
- Freedom to do what you want
- Freedom from painful anxiety
- A better relationship with money
- Freedom to live a life based on your values
- More confidence in your ability to manage money
- Less stress, which means better health
- Freedom to grow wealthy on your own terms

If you're ready to change your life for the better — to stop merely existing in this world rather than truly living — then it is time for you to take the next step. The sooner you start, the sooner you will see yourself journeying that road to financial freedom. It is my responsibility to guide you step by step to that dream lifestyle you want.

So, if you're ready to change your life, and move onto something that's even better, then it's time to download this book today. It's totally up to you to take back control of your life and actually win the rat race for a change. So, what are you waiting for? Now is the time to change your life for the better by letting us help you to gain financial freedom.

Chapter 1: The Building Blocks of Financial Freedom

Most goals should have a specific end date, but things aren't so simple when it comes to money. For one thing, your ultimate goal of financial freedom needs to be broken down into a lot of smaller goals. Not only that, you will have to live life in a very specific way in order to maintain those circumstances after you have acquired it.

Overwhelmed? Don't be, as it all starts simply by having a specific mindset.

Important Mindset Shifts to Start Accruing Wealth

There is nothing unique about finances. While it may be elusive to some people, it is really just a matter of mastering the fundamentals. Whether you're Jeff Bezos or you're the cleaning lady, the rules of the game are exactly the same: mastering the fundamentals and consistently applying them.

This is not just about saving up for a new car or for a fabulous vacation one day. Yes, savings is very important in the grand scheme of things, but saving just for the sake of saving is not always your best option. Your first goal is to make the most of your money, not just for today or the next few years, but for the remainder of your life. This requires a huge shift in perspective. You're in it for the long haul and that means that what you need for today may not be what is needed in 10 years or 20 or 50.

Have you ever heard of people who seem to have struck it rich overnight? Chances are you have. You might even have personally known a few of them. Some of them may have been positioned in high paying jobs where they could sock away a lot of cash whenever they wanted, but others may have started with little or nothing. They may have been the local garbage collector, the housekeeper, or a waitress at a nearby diner.

Aside from those who have acquired their wealth by winning the lottery, others have managed to achieve their money seemingly without effort. However, if you look closely, their imagined overnight success came after years of careful planning. There is nothing more important to your success than changing your mental mindset. You will have to switch from the common ideas that are the norm in today's society to something that will guarantee that you get improved results.

Essential Steps for Achieving Financial Freedom

1. Make a detailed plan

One of the first steps you must do is to create a plan. Your success should not be something you get by accident or by surprise. Each step of your path should be made and achieved by design. Rather than allowing things to just happen, start thinking about everything you do and any possible consequences that can occur.

Imagine designing your dream home. You've probably thought about it for years. You know every detail, down to the shape and design of each knob and fixture. If it's truly your dream house, you've already thought about what it will take to repair it when things go wrong, what colors to paint it and how often. You know which rooms to give your kids and every feature you'll have in your kitchen.

You have to take the same extra care when planning for your financial future. You're not thinking just for today but are planning for the future. How many years will it take for you to reach your goal and the kind of effort you will need to maintain it? With a detailed plan, you'll know what to do today, tomorrow, next month, next year, and each year after that. You'll keep doing this until you reach a point where your money will start to work for you.

2. Get out of the paycheck-to-paycheck mindset

We've been programmed from childhood to think in terms of survival. Perhaps it's human nature, but many of us who are struggling to survive tend to focus on the negatives. Even though events may not have automatically come to mind, it's easy to fall into the sky is falling approach to everything. The problem with this line of thinking is that it limits us. When you are concerned, your mind focuses on holding onto every penny you have, investment opportunities can easily pass you by because you're only thinking in the moment.

Wealthy people do not think this way. Because they have a plan, their minds are focused on the next step, which will automatically lead them to prosperity. Their minds are free to explore other possibilities, and they see opportunities all around them. They examine each one and process every aspect of it until they reach a breakthrough where they can see how to use it to grow what they have rather than holding onto everything they have earned.

3. **Don't always play it safe**

In line with the survival line of thinking is the need to seek security. Yes, money can bring you a level of security. You know that if you have enough money, you have a roof over your head, food in your stomach and clothes on your back. However, if your mind never looks beyond your safety net, you may miss many profitable opportunities. No one ever achieved financial independence while sitting on the fence. Playing it safe cuts you off from many avenues you can take to wealth.

This doesn't mean that you should throw caution to the wind. You still need to think things through and analyze every opportunity to make sure that it's a risk that will pay off in the end. Being a risk-taker doesn't mean being foolhardy. It means that you're going to have to step out on faith and believe in your decisions even when you don't know the outcome.

Courage has been defined as the willingness to take action when you cannot control the outcome. Take the time to read a few background stories of successful people that you admire, and you'll find the same pattern. They recognized an opportunity and took action, often before anyone else saw the potential. By the time others joined in, they were already well on their way to amassing great wealth.

4. **Stop thinking about spending and start thinking about saving**

This is a mindset that's quite ingrained. If your parents taught you well, then chances are you didn't spend every penny of your allowance when you were a kid. You might have had to save up for that new bike or computer game. Sadly, many young people grow up spending every last penny they have for the things they want. In most cases, the things they want don't last for very long. So, when those things are gone, so is their money.

The average American household spends 110% of their income. When they overspend, they usually find themselves deep in debt with credit cards and loans from friends and family members. If you have a spendthrift attitude, your attempts to acquire wealth will inevitably dig a hole for yourself that will be almost impossible to get out of.

There have been numerous studies that show that you need to save between 20–30% of your income to reach the point where your money will actually work for you. Taking 20% of your income and setting it aside and then living off the rest is not that hard. Once you make this adjustment, you're not likely to even notice the difference.

5. Stop hoping and start doing

Hope is a powerful motivator, but there will always comes a time when you need to take action. You need to stop thinking about what you want to do and become proactive. Even the smallest step in the right direction can be rewarding.

Most people do not realize that they are paralyzed by hope. They spend their time talking and sharing their ideas, but they rarely get beyond that point. Rather than spending your energy sharing your plans with others, start gathering what you need to execute your plan.

Just like everything else in life, nothing we say or do happens without it first being a thought. If you've developed bad financial habits in the past, they were started with your thinking. So, in order to gain financial freedom, it is necessary for you to change the way you think about money. By changing your thoughts, you can accomplish great things in an amazingly short amount of time. You'll start off slowly at first, but gradually your plans will pick up momentum and as the time passes you see small successes along your path, you'll start to feel more confident and you'll see your freedom just beyond that light at the end of the tunnel.

How to Set Your Financial Goals

Most people do not fully understand money or how it works. They think that having cash on hand is security and cannot grasp how saving it may not be the best choice for them. Anything you do to increase your financial security has to have a goal. If you are saving money, you need to have a goal for that. Money is not the end-all of anything you do. It is the means to an end. If money is never used for any purpose, you end up either wasting it on frivolous things or hoarding it. In the end, you may leave this earth and all your money behind for someone else to use.

Take a long hard look at your goals and try to determine where your money should be going. Actually, sitting down and putting pen to paper can be a little scary, but it brings you face to face with your financial realities.

When you're laying out what you plan to do with your money and setting your goals, it can be kind of cathartic. But before you do anything, make sure your boots are firmly planted on the ground. Without clearly defined goals, you may end up jumping ship and splurging the first chance you get. It could be very easy to end up watching that wealth as it slips away, buried under a mountain of debt. So, when setting your goals, start with a realistic but flexible plan.

What you might want today may not be what you want later in life, make sure you have some wiggle room to work with.

- **Determine how much money you have to start with.** It doesn't matter if your goals are short or long-term, you need to know your starting point. Be realistic about how much you have to work with. If you don't, it is quite likely you'll work your way to the bottom of your wallet before you reach your final destination. Remember, your goal is to stop living from paycheck to paycheck, so you don't want to start blind.

Take some time to sit down and get a realistic look at your current financial situation. Your starting point should consist of 1) how much money you have on hand and in your bank accounts, IRAs, or investments; include physical assets that you may have already paid off. 2) List all of the debts you still have outstanding. Consider credit card balances, mortgages, student loans, child support or any other financial obligations that you have to meet.

Take the total amount you owe and deduct it from your total assets to get your net worth. This is your starting point. Don't worry if this number is in the negative, the goal of reading this book is to change that.

- **Create a budget.** Now that you know what you're worth financially, you have a starting point and you can figure out a budget. Your budget will be a detailed outline of all the expenses that you have and how much you will pay towards them every month.

- **Make sure you cover everything.** That includes that $10.00/month video streaming service that you take for granted. In addition to obvious expenses, include utilities, insurance policies, food, gas, and entertainment. Don't leave anything out. If you're not sure of what to include on the list, go back over the last few months of receipts and take a look. This list will be the foundation of your budget.

Take a look at your starting figure. If you don't like it, then go back through your list to see if you can cut some of those expenses. What can you eliminate? Cable? Streaming? Subscription accounts? You might even be able to forego eating out and opt to do more cooking at home.

This doesn't mean that you have to give up on your good times, you just have to be willing to sacrifice a little to get better returns. Once you've decided what you can do without, you'll see that final number getting larger. You now have a budget!

Now that you know how much you have to work with, you can start setting realistic goals.

- **Set practical goals.** Financial goals are not the same for everyone, so no one can tell you what to shoot for. However, there are some practical goals you might want to consider. You can always add to them later if you want. The most common goals you'll find people set are:

  o Establishing an emergency fund
  o Getting out of debt

- Planning for retirement
- Buying a home or a car
- Taking a dream vacation

You can choose for yourself which ones should be addressed first, but as long as the first three are addressed you should be able to find the security you're looking for. Follow these basic suggestions to help you get started.

Goal 1: Establishing an emergency fund. If you've done your budget well, you'll at least have a few dollars to dedicate to an emergency fund. In the beginning, it may not be much. Maybe $5 or $10 each paycheck. However, if you are consistent, you'll be amazed at just how much you can accumulate with a steady deposit of a few bucks into your account.

You decide just how much money you want to have in your emergency fund. No one can tell you how much you need, but a general guideline is three to six months' worth of living expenses should be set aside. If you have good job security that may be enough, but if you're on a precarious footing with your job, then you might decide on a little more.

Goal 2: Pay Down Your Debt. It is easy to get bogged down in bills every month and it can be very discouraging to watch your account bleed out every payday. Some people see money as electricity, and they are merely the wire it passes through. It goes out as fast, if not faster, than its coming in.

The best way to solve this problem is to take aim on those bills and pay them off. Being-debt free may feel like an impossible task, but if you're willing to make a few sacrifices in the beginning, even a few extra dollars added to each payment will start to see that balance slowly begin to. Just make sure that you don't spend any of your emergency fund money in the interim.

Goal 3: Planning for retirement. You want to think about your future, even if you're a long way from its reality. If you haven't thought much about this yet, then you're not alone. If you love your job and can't imagine life without it, then maybe you can get by, but by and large, the majority of people want to see a day when they do not have to get up and trudge to work all day. They want to spend their later years doing the things they love and making the most out of their lives.

The sooner you start this plan, the easier it will be to get to that final day at work when you can claim your life back. It doesn't matter how old you are, it's never too early to start planning for retirement. If you have a job that offers a nice 401(k) plan all the better. However, even if they don't, you can still set aside money for those later years on your own. Your future self will thank you profusely for it.

Setting Your Short-Term and Long-Term Goals

Now for the fun part. Once you've got the adult things out of the way, it's time to think about supporting the kid in you. This is where you decide how you will use that accumulated wealth to enhance your quality of life. Think about the kinds of things that will give you enjoyment and satisfaction in life.

It doesn't matter what your goals are, it's time to start making a list to help you to categorize them in order of importance. Start by making a list of all the things you want to do, then separate them into different categories:

1.   **Short-term**: goals that can be filled within just a few years. Vacations, buying a car, or taking a gourmet cooking class.

2.   **Long-term**: goals that may take you 10 years or more to achieve. Buying a house or developing rental property.

By detailing your heart's desire on paper, you put them front and center in your life. Make sure when you write down your goals that you also set an estimated timeline for achieving it. The timeline is what will motivate you to move forward, do the necessary research and take the steps to achieve it without procrastinating.

10 Ways to Get Out of Debt ASAP

The fun part of budgeting and financial planning is in your dreams. But if you're serious about obtaining financial freedom you need to get out of debt first. This can be difficult when you consider that most people today are in debt to the tune of nearly $25,000. That's a lot of bills to pay.

Because people tend to spend more than they earn, the accumulated debt in most cases is the result of credit use to make up the difference. If you want to find the wealth you're looking for, you can no longer hide behind your credit to get the things you need. All it takes is one disaster or unfortunate event and you'll be well on your way to bankruptcy.

1. **Don't just pay the minimum payment.** Take a look at the interest rate on your credit card statement. In most cases, it is 15% or higher. At that rate, if you pay only the minimum payment amount each month, it could take you years to pay it off. This is one of the main reasons why people are unable to see their way clear of credit card bills, but interest rates can be the bane of your existence in other loans too. Think about all the interest you're paying for your student loans, personal loans, or other forms of debt.

- The best way to pay these bills down faster is to pay more than the minimum payment. You'll not only cut down on the interest you pay, but the additional money you add will help to reduce the principal amount owed speeding up the payment process.

- Before you completely pay off your debt, check to make sure that your creditor is not going to charge you any prepayment penalties for paying it off early.

2. **Use the snowball method.** If you can find a way to pay more than the minimum monthly payment, you can use the snowball method to pay off your debts. This will not only get the bills paid, but it will boost your sense of accomplishment along the way.

o List all of your debts from the smallest to the largest. Use all your excess funds to pay off the smallest debt first and make minimum monthly payments on all the other ones. Once the smallest bill is paid off, then take that extra cash and pay it towards the next smallest bill on the list until that one is paid in full.

o In essence, you are snowballing all of your extra money and pushing towards the total amount you owe until you reach a point when you can say you are debt-free.

3. **Get an extra job.** If you can see your way clear to pick up a few extra dollars with an additional job you can actually put a lot more cash in your pocket to pay off those extra bills. It doesn't have to be a regular job where you have to punch a clock every day. Nearly everyone has some specialized skill or talent that they can tap into. Picking up a few weekend jobs a month or freelance assignments can go far in putting extra cash in your pocket.

4. **Downsize your life.** If you're really determined, you can cut your expenses down to the absolute minimum, until all your bills are paid in full. This means you will eliminate all extra spending and just use enough money to get by. If this thought is making your heart race too fast, relax a little. This type of budget is not meant to be a lifetime decision but will only be exercised until you become debt-free.

5. **Have a garage/yard sale.** Everyone has a lot of stuff they no longer have any use for. Take some time and go through your garage, closets, basements, and attics to see what you've got stashed away.

You know the saying, "one man's trash is another man's treasure." If you find things in your home that you no longer use and have no realistic expectations of using them in the future, you should have no problem coming up with things to sell.

a.   If you don't have time to set up a yard sale, consider taking your things to a consignment shop or sell them online on sites like eBay, Facebook, or Craigslist.

6.   **Negotiate a lower interest rate.** If you're struggling with excessively high interest rates, it may be possible to negotiate for a lower rate. Many people do not think to make such a request, but many credit companies are happy to oblige, especially if you have a good relationship with them.

7.   **Transfer your balance.** If you have one credit card with an extremely high bill and you're paying high interest rates on top of that, you may be able to transfer the remaining balance to another card with a lower interest rate. There are even some cards that offer a 0% interest rate for the first 18 months. With that kind of kick, you'll have a lot of extra cash to throw at those bills.

8.   **Use unexpected money to pay down debt.** Throughout the year, you may receive additional unexpected income. For example, you might receive an end-of-the-year bonus from your employer, or you may get a nice fat tax refund check. Perhaps a rich uncle has left you a tidy little sum or you get a raise. Whatever the case, it is not money that you have dedicated to your budgetary expenses. Use that money to pay down your debt and you'll be well ahead of the game.

9. **Stop unnecessary spending**. More often than not, the credit card balance doesn't go down because you keep adding to it. Taking the time to examine how you use your credit card can give you a good picture of your spending habits. By looking back over your past expenditures, you can decide for yourself if the debt was really worth it. Maybe you could have settled for a regular cup of coffee rather than a mocha Frappuccino. Brown bagging it to work can keep you from going out to eat saving you tons of money. By eliminating expensive habits, you can cut your overall expenses down to something that is much more manageable.

10. **Avoid temptation**. We all have things that are hard to resist. Still, you can almost guarantee that with all the marketing and advertising going on around you every day, the carrot that society is dangling in front of your eyes every day will tempt you. When you're trying to pay down debt, it is best to try to avoid those temptations wherever you go. If you're drawn into your favorite restaurant on your way home from work every day, try taking a different route. If you see the same tempting commercial on when you watch TV, consider changing the channel or at least getting up and walking out of the room during commercial breaks.

The bottom line is *you have a choice*. You can continue to take the easy road and just stick your head in the sand, pretending you do not see your financial situation, or you can face your debt issues head on. Whether you choose to do it now or are faced to deal with it later, you're going to have to pay your bills. It's better to do it on your own terms.

The main thing to remember is that there is a way out, but don't expect a miracle. With your plans to achieve financial freedom, it's going to take a little hustle on your part, but if you do, you'll be richly rewarded for all your hard work in the end.

Chapter 2: How to Budget the Right Way

Building good credit is essential to your financial future. While it is possible to live in this world without credit, it is not easy. But, getting out of debt and reestablishing your credit is not easy either. It takes careful planning and becoming fully aware off every dollar you spend. The only way to get out of the quagmire is by careful budgeting, but even that can get a little confusing. There are so many different plans for budgeting that it can be overwhelming to know what to do.

The problem is that creating a budget is not as cut and dry as you might believe. Just like not all credit habits are the same, not all approaches to correcting your financial situation will be suitable for you. Yes, the ultimate goal remains consistent: you want to pay down debt, build up a little nest egg, or work towards a major purchase. But reality dictates that there are many roads you can take to get there.

How to Find a Budget That Works for You

Before you can decide on the method that you will apply to your finances, think about the factors that are currently affecting your life. Clearly, a single person living alone will not have as much to worry about as one who has a family to support. You also have to dedicate time to creating a budget and consider the resources you have at your disposal. Below are several budgeting methods you can consider. Read them through and see which one rings true for you. This will help you to determine where you lie on the spectrum so you can plan an effective approach to budgeting going forward.

When you know your starting point, deciding the route to take is much easier. You know what you have to work with and where you want to end up. All that's left is to draw a line on your road map.

1. **Know your values.** Your values consist of what matters to you, the things in your life that you feel you can't live without. Obviously, food, clothing, and shelter would be on the top of this list. Values may differ from person to person. The point is that understanding your values will help you to prioritize what's most important in your budget.

2. **Set your goals.** Your values will give you clear directions on what you should be striving for. Think about what you want your money to do for you in the future, but don't just write down one single long-term goal. Break it up into workable steps. What would you like to accomplish in the next month, three months, six months, a year, three years, five years, 10 years?

3. **Know your income.** How much money do you bring home each pay period – after taxes? This will be the money you will use to determine your spending allowance. You only want to include money that you receive on a regular basis and that you KNOW is coming.

4. **Know your expenses.** Look over your credit card statements, bank records, and store receipts. You can divide your expenses into two categories – fixed and flexible expenses. Fixed expenses would be your rent or mortgage, car payment, credit card bills, and student loans.

Flexible expenses are a little harder to figure out. These include things like food, clothing, entertainment, etc. The cost varies from one month to the next. You may have to calculate the total amount over several months and then come up with a reasonable average.

Don't forget about additional expenses that are easily forgotten. These are those costs that you do not pay with regularity; taxes, insurance, subscriptions, etc.

Now, you have all the tools you need to create a workable budget that will help you to meet your needs.

Now comes the part when you have to decide what method will work best for you.

6 Must-Know Budgeting Methods to Never Lose Track of Money Again

As long as the fundamentals of budgeting are covered — tracking expenses, managing income — you have a little leeway in choosing the budgeting method that works for you. If one of them looks like a good fit, then go for it. There's no harm in switching to another one if you find it doesn't quite meet your needs.

1. The Line-Item Budget

The line-item budget is designed for those who have problems with major spending issues. People who use it are those that seriously need to get out of debt and have no problem with putting all of their expenses into workable categories.

This system requires you to categorize your expenses. You can create as many categories as you need to: household expenses, credit card debt, transportation costs, food, clothing, utilities, grooming, you get the idea. Under each category, list all of the expenses you have to pay.

Create three columns, estimated spending, actual spending, and whatever is left over. When you compare each of these columns, you will be able to measure your progress after each pay period.

Next to each item, assign a dollar amount to be paid monthly. As you make each payment, make a note of it and deduct the amount from the total due. It might be helpful to create an additional bill for incidentals, that way, nothing is left out.

This budgeting method is perfect for the person that has the time and the resources to figure out a lot of details and the dedication to do the extra work that is involved.

2. The 50/30/20 Budget

The 50/30/20 budget has guidelines that aren't as meticulous. However, with the 50/30/20 budget, you dedicate 50% of your income to necessary expenses, 30% to things you want, and 20% to savings.

This method is ideal for those who are not comfortable with a strict budget or they don't have a lot of time to dedicate to doing a line-item budget. Still, it is flexible enough that you know exactly how much you can put away and how much you have to spend on your daily needs. The model should be flexible enough to fit in with your lifestyle.

3. Pay Yourself First

The pay yourself first model takes money from your income and put it into a savings account before you pay for anything else. Even though you pay yourself first, you will still need to know just how much money you need to meet your expenses so that you have enough to cover them.

This method works well for those who find themselves at the end of the month wondering where all of their money has gone. At the same time, it doesn't require you to stick to a strict dollar accounting.

It also works well with those who have an inconsistent monthly income. First, take the average of the last six months of income, then total all of your expenses for the same period, and then subtract the expenses from the income. The remainder is what you can dedicate to your savings.

4. The Envelope System

There is another system that works with a little tighter pull on the purse strings. It works well for those who need a little more discipline to get the job done. The envelope system helps you to cut back on spending too much on non-essentials without having to keep track of every penny you spend. It is a basic cash-based approach to budgeting.

Determine a spending limit for each expense. For example, you could create individual budgets for groceries, clothing, and entertainment. At the start of each month, divide all of your money into these smaller budget categories and place it into labeled envelopes. Anytime you need to purchase something from one of those categories, you pay for it out of that envelope. When the envelope is empty, you have exhausted your budget and there is no more money to make any more purchases until the next payday.

This method works well for those who struggle to control their spending habits or are relying too heavily on credit or debit cards to pay for things. They don't realize how much they are spending until all of their money is gone.

5. Zero-Sum Budget

Then there is the zero-based budget, which is particularly good for anyone who has a tendency to overspend without realizing it. With this plan, you will know exactly how every dollar you spend is being used. In other words, every dollar must have an intended purpose before it leaves your hands, you must account for every penny in order for it to work well.

The system works exactly the way it sounds. On the last day of the month, your budget should always equal zero. So, if at the end of the month, you have money left over, you must stop and find a home for that money.

It works for those people who usually have a little extra cash at the end of the month. Without giving the money a job to do, the tendency to use it for unnecessary things can be a problem. It forces you to stop and think practically about how best to use your funds so that they push you closer to your goals.

6. The No-Budget Budget

This method requires you to be aware of your spending habits. Rather than worrying about how much is being spent in each of your categories, you spend based on your values and what's most important to you.

It works well for those who may already be pretty frugal and somewhat disciplined about the money they spend.

Start by creating an outline for everything that you feel comfortable spending your money on. Anything that is not in line with what you feel is important or essential should not make it on this list.

For example, you might be someone who prefers traveling and taking a vacation once or twice a year. Any extra money you have after your needs are met can be dedicated to travel.

Some people may prefer to dedicate their money to their pets, others may want to invest in the stock market, while others may be thinking about becoming an entrepreneur. Your discretionary money can pretty much be dedicated to anything that you think is important and can enhance your life.

Which Budget Is Right for You?

As you can see, there are several different ways to budget for your future. While the end-goal is the same with all of them, only one will fit with your lifestyle and your way of managing money.

To decide which system will work best for you, there are a few things you need to keep in mind.

• How much time do you have to monitor your budget? Some methods are relatively easy and do not require a lot of detailed record-keeping. But others may require elaborate record-keeping with numerous Excel spreadsheets and constantly tracking every penny you spend. If you don't have a lot of time to dedicate to such extensive record-keeping, you might want to start working a budget that has a little more give and take.

• You should also think about how often you should monitor your budget. Those who are pretty confident that their budget is on the right track might review their results on a monthly basis, while others may choose to view it once or twice a year. If you're still trying to get the balance just right, you might be more inclined to review it on a weekly basis or even after every purchase.

At the very least, having a budget allows you to approach life with confidence. You know that you have a plan and a direction you want to go in. Every time you pay a bill, you get a sense of pride that you are one step closer to your goals, and that is worth money in the bank.

7 Ways to Make Budgeting More Enjoyable

There are many benefits to learning how to budget properly, but many of us are gun shy from those arduous days from our middle and high school classrooms. However, with just a few little tips, those boring math classes can be brought to life and you can find out just how much fun you can have crunching those numbers.

1.   Take Advantage of Modern Tech

If you really aren't good at numbers, take advantage of modern tech. There are plenty of excellent applications that can help you to get your budgeting done with minimal effort. Each one has its own set of features that can be applied to your situation. After a careful search and analysis of the available options, it is possible to find one that will fit your needs.

2.   Know Your Goals

The work becomes a lot more interesting when you know why you're doing it. When you start by establishing some clear-cut goals, even if they are small ones, it gives meaning to what you want to do. If you set both long and short-term goals, you'll have certain milestones to achieve and once you've mastered a few of them, you'll find yourself motivated to push forward.

Start by setting up a few easy ones that you know you can achieve, and then watch the magic as it happens. There is nothing more motivating and encouraging than success. The larger goals can be broken up into small steps. Each milestone you pass will help you to see that you are making progress even if the end is months or years away.

3. Give Yourself Rewards

The main reason we do anything is for the rewards. We go to work for the reward of the paycheck, we study hard in school for the reward of a good grade, we do our best in competition for the reward of the prize, and we struggle through relationships for the reward of a happy family life. It just stands to reason that you will work harder when there is something rewarding at the end of the fight.

There are all types of rewards you might give yourself, just make sure that your reward is in line with your goals. You could treat yourself to a night on the town after a completing a full month of budgeting, set aside a little money for a vacation or a weekend getaway, or reward yourself with a new outfit or a pair of shoes.

The main point is that you acknowledge what you have accomplished and be happy about it. Perfection is a good goal to reach, but if it is offered at the expense of your mental and emotional stability, you may reach your goal but there won't be much satisfaction in it.

4. It's Not Just About You

Even if you have small children, letting everyone in the family be a part of the solution takes a lot of the burden off of you and can make it much more rewarding. Some people turn budgeting into a game by allowing the children to compete by seeing who can either make the most money on odd jobs or who can save the most.

Just as rewards will work well for you, they'll do wonders to motivate the youngest ones in the family: a trip to the local candy store, something from the ice-cream truck, or a day at the park (that's free!). Remember, a reward for your kids is also a reward for you. It'll be easier to achieve your goals and it will be a major boost to your children's self-esteem. They'll learn good money managing habits and they'll feel like part of the solution rather than the problem.

5. Become More Self-Sufficient

Saving money is not just about shifting dollars from one place to another. While you can save that way, it is a lot more fun to learn creative ways to acquire the things you need without shelling out a lot of cash. There is nothing more rewarding than heading out to your backyard to pick your vegetables for dinner than finding them at your local supermarket.

And the best part of it is that everyone in the family can take part. Your children will learn a valuable and precious skill that will last them a lifetime, and you'll save money at the same time. Once they taste the difference in the foods you grow, they may not want to eat store-bought food ever again.

There are a lot of things you can do to save money. In addition to growing your own food, you can create your own cleaning supplies, learn to sew your own clothes, or even make your own hair products.

In fact, if you do well, you may be able to parlay some of that into a side business that will help you to keep you on budget too. What can be better than that?

6. Think Differently About Money

Learn to think of money in a different way. Chances are, you've seen money as a source of stress and anxiety for a while now. The need for money has caused many to fall so far into debt, it's no wonder so many people see it in a negative light.

Now, as you begin to see your money working for you rather than against you, it is possible to view it as a means to an end. As you learn how to prioritize your spending and you see its effects as you pass one milestone after another, you'll see money more as a tool you can utilize to your advantage.

7. Plan for Early Retirement

The sooner you start planning for retirement, the sooner you'll be able to see money as a way to make it happen. Think about all the things you can have if you are able to retire early. The time you can spend with your family, the vacations you'll enjoy, the time you'll have to do the things you love, and the stress-free life you will lead.

While budgeting may be a necessity, it doesn't have to be painful or stressful. By coming up with creative ways to make it more interesting, you can ensure your success. Creative budgeting can be a great way to motivate your whole family, friends, and neighbors to help you to achieve your goals without losing your heart in the process.

7 Important Steps for Building Good Credit

Bad credit can be the bane of anyone's existence. It can prevent you from renting a decent place to live, stop you from purchasing a home, cut off your means of education, and it might even be the reason you couldn't get a good job. If you have bad credit, then you already know what this feels like.

It can be very exciting to get that first credit card. Every purchase you make, every late payment, starts to develop into a picture that becomes very hard to erase. Being able to use credit responsibly is one sure way of securing your financial future.

Sadly though, this lesson comes a little too late for most people, and they end up having to rebuild their credit and recover from some painful decisions they have made in the past.

The good news though, is that no matter how bad your credit is today, there are ways to rebuild it and restore your good name. It may take time, but by applying some very basic principles you can establish a good credit history, one that you can be proud of.

Whether you're trying to restore your credit or you're just starting out, keep these little tips in mind to protect your image and make sure that your credit doesn't suffer from bad decisions in the future.

1.   Never Borrow More Than You Can Afford

You received your credit because you were viewed as creditworthy, so don't start off using it with bad spending habits. Make sure that when you use your card you only use it for things you can afford. It can be difficult to resist the temptation to buy things on credit that you can already buy without it, but it is a powerful signal to future creditors that you are being responsible. You'll be glad you were frugal when you can later get those big-ticket items you couldn't get before.

This is also true when it comes to taking out loans. Only borrow what you know for a fact you can pay back within a reasonable amount of time. Take a little time to look over your budget so that you know exactly what you can afford to pay on a monthly basis. If the loan payment amount exceeds that number, don't be afraid to walk away.

2. Don't Use All of Your Credit

Just because a creditor gives you a maximum limit, it does not give you carte blanche to use it all. When you max out your credit cards, creditors view it as irresponsible, especially if you're not in the habit of paying off your bill in full every month. Lenders notice that borrowers who max out their credit are usually the same ones that have difficulty paying off their balance. Try to keep your balance at around 40% of your credit limit to maintain a good credit score.

3. Don't Get a Lot of Credit Cards

Opening up too much new credit too soon can be very damaging to your credit.
Try sticking to only one credit card at a time. Establish a good rating with that one and use it for a couple of years before trying to apply for a new one. Your credit rating will remain strong if you don't race out of the gate but start building it up slow and steadily.

4. Pay Your Balance in Full Every Month

You've probably heard that it's important to pay your balance in full every month. If you are only charging what you can afford to pay, this is not a problem. When you are careful with your spending and can pay off your balance each month, you show your creditors that you are responsible. As a result, you'll end up with a higher credit score.

5. Pay on Time

One of the most important things you can do when it comes to paying your bills is to *pay on time*. It is important to make it a habit to pay everything on time so that it doesn't have a chance to negatively affect your score. Any bill that has the possibility of becoming delinquent and end up being sent to a collection agency can harm your credit.

6. Manage Balances Properly

There will be times when you have to carry a balance on some big-ticket items. If you find that you can't pay the balance in full at the end of the month, make sure that you pay a significant amount so that you are paying more than interest payments on the debt owed.

Always try to pay more than the minimum payment each month until you pay your balance down. When you do that and keep your balance owed to less than 30% of your credit limit, you protect your credit and can maintain a relatively high score.

7. Allow Your Accounts to Mature

Having good credit can be a good thing, but the longer you have it, the better. As your accounts mature it looks good on a credit report. When you keep the oldest accounts active, they give your credit image a boost. Keep in mind that if you close any account, it may take several years before it drops off of your record, so leave them open, even if you don't plan to use them. This will show creditors that you are not relying on it to get by.

Establishing good credit is extremely important for anyone who is seeking financial freedom. While there are several ways to reach that goal, establishing a good budget, and sticking to it is a surefire key to success. But budgeting doesn't have to mean months of drudgery and deprivation as some people have been led to believe. If you do it the right way, find a plan that works well with your lifestyle and personality, you're well on your way to discovering the freedom that comes from managing your money well.

It's not enough to have a good budget; you need to know how to implement it properly. That includes knowing how to use credit wisely. Setting up a good financial future, should not feel like a punishment, but should feel uplifting and rewarding. By following these very basic guidelines you can find success along the way and the big pay-off years down the line.

Chapter 3: Investing 101

Learning how to manage your money is a big step towards gaining financial freedom, but once you've succeeded, you're only half-way there. The reality is that finding wealth and financial security rarely comes from good management of credit and savings accounts.

Those two features can put you in a better financial position, but they don't erase the fact that you still need to work for your money. A savvy financial planner understands that the transition from working for your money to having your money work for you is a huge step. To get your money to work for you means that you have to invest.

Types of Investments to Add to Your Portfolio

There are a wide variety of investment options available for anyone who is willing to take the risk. Understanding your level of risk tolerance can make a major difference in which investment tools you choose to make. When making investment decisions, you need to decide if you're willing to invest for the long haul or you want a quick return and make a short-term investment. For most people, the first line of investment options for the long-term are either in stocks or bonds, but there's a wide variety of options to choose from.

1. **Stocks**

In its most basic definition, a stock is a purchase of a small portion of a specific company. When you buy a share, you are actually buying a percentage of the business' potential earnings and assets. When a business sells shares in its company, it is doing so in order to raise capital to invest in its own operations. As an investor, you can buy or sell your shares to improve your own financial portfolio.

When the value of the stock increases, an investor can then sell his shares at a higher price than what he bought it for and make a profit. Another way to make money in stocks is by purchasing stocks that pay dividends. Dividends are distributions of earnings given out periodically to investors. You can choose to invest in dividend stocks or growth stocks.

With dividend stocks, you will receive a regular distribution of earnings without the need to sell your interest in the business. Dividends can be paid out monthly, quarterly, bi-annually, annually or on some other payment schedule. Most companies that pay out dividends are pretty well-established and in most cases are considered safe.

Growth stocks are also shares in companies that are expected to see a certain amount of growth. They don't pay out any dividends, so you don't get a regular payout for owning them. The only way to turn a profit with a growth stock is to sell your shares in the business.

There is a certain level of risk with both options. Dividend stocks are usually the preferred choice for those with a low-risk tolerance. Growth stocks are a little less predictable but that doesn't mean they are less stable. There are times when the profits from a growth stock can actually be more rewarding than dividends.

If you're thinking of investing in the stock market, it just makes sense for you to compare the two, learn your level of risk tolerance, and decide which type works best for you.

2. Bonds

When you purchase a bond, you are technically lending money to the issuer and will receive a certain amount of interest for allowing them access to your funds.

For the most part, bonds are believed to be much safer than stocks, but the possibilities for grand returns is rare. You also have an additional risk to worry about. Just like with any company that extends loans to others, there is always a risk of the borrower going into default. Government bonds are usually safer because they are backed by the "full faith and credit" of the United States federal government. Next to government bonds in safety are state and city bonds. Corporate bonds come with more risk but are considered to be the third safest choice.

Investors earn profit from regular interest payments from the borrower, which is usually paid once or twice each year with the principal being paid back on the maturity date. Bonds are fixed-income investments, which means the amount of the investment is fixed and does not change.

3. Mutual Funds

When you purchase a mutual fund, you are investing in a larger number of stocks with one single transaction. The funds collect money from a wide range of investors and then invest that money into select stocks, bonds, or assets.

These investment instruments are found and selected based on a set strategy. For example, one fund may only be a specific type of stocks or bonds, while others may have a different set of parameters. One fund may choose to work only with international stocks while another may want to focus on technology or the sciences.

Profits are made when the selected list of investments goes up in price. The money received could be in the form of dividends or interest. Periodically these are dispersed to the customer. Also, when the investments actually do increase in value, owners are free to sell their interest for a profit.

4.   Index Funds

An index fund is one type of mutual fund which passively tracks all the stocks in a particular index. This type of fund doesn't use a fund manager to choose which stocks to invest in. Rather, the decision is based on all the stocks in that particular index. For example, one well-known index fund is the Standard & Poor's 500, which has the goal of matching the performance of the S&P 500 by holding shares in every one of the companies listed in that index.

One of the biggest advantages of investing in index funds is their low cost. Because there is no need to have a live person to manage the fund, you save money.

Index funds earn money through either dividend or interest payments made periodically. They can also make money when the value of their investment increases. Investors can sell their share in the fund when the price goes up.

5. Exchange Traded Funds (ETFs)

One type of index fund is an exchange-traded fund or an ETF. ETFs strive to copy the performance of a specific kind of index. Because they are also not actively managed, they are also much cheaper than mutual funds.

You can purchase ETFs on the regular stock exchange and sell them the same way. The price will fluctuate up and down throughout the day, just like regular stocks. However, both mutual and index funds have a fixed price that is only adjusted at the end of each trading day.

Profits are earned the same as with all other funds. Some ETFs pay dividends or interest rates, but you can also make money when the fund increases in value and you sell it at a profit.

6. Options

An option is simply a contract to buy or sell a particular stock at a pre-determined price or on a set date. Even though you enter into a contract, you are not required to buy or sell the stock, so you have the flexibility to decline the offer if you choose to. The contract only gives you an "option" to make such a transaction. You also have the option to sell the contract to another investor or let it expire.

An options contract allows you to lock in a particular stock at a lower price. If you are right, you are opting in on a chance to purchase the stock at a later date at a more favorable price than the rest of the market. If your predictions are wrong, you lose only the money you invested in buying the contract and walk away.

You will have to open a brokerage account with either your bank or an investment firm. Once the account is opened and funded, you can start making your investment.

However, you have to be very careful with the fees. Some firms will charge monthly fees while others will charge for every transaction. When calculating your profits, make sure that once you've made your decision, the profits you claim are not eaten up by the costs of making that transaction.

Understanding the Bond Market

Before you purchase a bond, you need to do a little research. There are loads of online resources that will help you to find the best bonds to invest in. Look for sites that will break down all of the information on the different securities, any news related to their performance, analysis, and other vital information that can help you to make a decision. Some of the most frequently used sites include Investopedia, Morningstar, Yahoo, and the Finance Bond Center.

As an individual investor, you cannot personally invest in the bond market. You will have to enlist the aid of an institutional investor. Most do this through their employee pension fund, their banks, an endowment fund, or an investment banker. If you don't have any one of these at your disposal, your next step would be to find an asset manager to make the investment for you.

There are three groups that are active in the bond market.

Issuers: Those that develop, register, and/or sell bonds on the market. These could be corporations or they could be from a governmental agency. We are probably most familiar with US Treasury bonds, which are issued by the Treasury Department, but there are other agencies that also issue bonds. Most bonds issued from the government will reach maturity after 10 years.

Underwriters: A group that evaluates the risks of each of the bonds. They buy securities from the issuers and then resells them to the buyers for a profit.

Participants: Participants buy bonds as loans to the various entities. The loans are extended for the length of the security and receive the face value of the bond once it reaches its maturity date.

Grades are issued by a bond rating agency and usually come in the form of a letter grade. For example, a "AAA" rating is considered very high quality and is least likely to go into default. A "BBB" rating is considered to be a medium risk, and anything that is a BB or lower is considered a high-risk investment opportunity.

Understanding the Stock Market

The stock market is where you buy shares in publicly traded companies. Like bonds, there are different types of stocks: common stocks, options, and futures.

The primary role of the stock market is to bring buyers and sellers together in a controlled environment. The market ensures that all securities are traded fairly, honestly, and with transparency. They keep trade between investors and corporations above board.

The stock market has two separate components. The first is set aside for new businesses offering initial public offerings or IPOs for trade. Underwriters set the initial price of securities for sale. IPOs tend to be higher risk investments as most of these corporations have not yet proven their worth.

The second component is for trading equities for the more established businesses. This is where the majority of trading on the stock market takes place.

There are several different stock exchanges, each one offering different securities to trade.

Nasdaq: This is an online electronic exchange that lists the securities issued from companies with a smaller capitalization. Stocks on the Nasdaq includes companies trading in a wide range of industries, including consumer goods, services, utilities, healthcare, and technology.

New York Stock Exchange: The NYSE trades some of the oldest and largest public companies in existence. You have probably heard of the Dow Jones Industrial Average (DJIA), which consists of the top 30 largest companies on the NYSE. These are also the oldest and most referred to indexes in the world.

American Stock Exchange: Initially, it was used for trading completely new asset classes. Today, it is the exchange used for buying and selling ETFs.

There are several distinct differences between the bond market and the stock market. The stock market has a central place of trade where investors of all sorts can buy and sell their interests, where the bond market does not. Also, there is a difference in risk levels between the two. Those who choose to invest in the stock market are likely exposed to a higher level of risk than those who invest in the bond market.

Bonds, however, are more likely to be affected by inflation and interest rates. When there is an increase in interest rates, the prices of bonds tend to drop. On the other hand, if the interest rates are high, the value of the bond itself can be deflated.

Credit risks are also something you need to carefully consider. Purchasing a bond from a company with a poor credit leaves you open to a potential default. In most cases, the issuer may not even be able to make the minimum interest payments on your investment and you could lose a lot more.

Some of the safest investment options to start with are US Treasury bonds. You are less likely to experience a default, but that doesn't mean they are 100% risk-free. They are still susceptible to price volatility over the life of the loan.

Tips on Choosing the Right Stocks for You

Your choice of stocks to trade will depend on several factors. 1) your experience, 2) how much you have to invest, 3) and your actual investment strategy.

There are several strategies to consider: day trading, position trading or long-term trading. It is important to note that your trading plan is not a fixed strategy, as it needs to be dynamic and flexible enough to adapt to a constantly changing marketplace. Later, as you begin trading and observing your successes and failures, you'll become wiser in your decisions, recognize your strengths and weaknesses and learn to utilize that new knowledge more effectively.

Before you begin:

1. Know your goals. What do you hope to accomplish with your financial portfolio? Those who are looking to generate an income will look at low-growth firms in stable industries like utilities, REITs (Real Estate Investment Trusts), and partnerships. If you have a clear picture of your risk tolerance and how you will manage it, you will be looking to preserve your capital by investing in premium blue-chip stocks.

2. If you're more interested in preserving capital, then you might focus your attention on those companies that go through various life cycle stages and ranging market caps.

3. All stocks will go up and down in price, but they won't all rise at the same time. By investing in a wider range of stocks, you'll have a better chance of generating a consistent amount of income with no significant downsides to deal with.

4. Be observant. When investing in stocks, you are always learning. Stay up to date on all current market events. Make it a habit to read blogs, study magazines, and keep abreast of the latest financial news. You should do this on a daily basis.

5. Finding the right company. Start by tracking the performance of a chosen industry and then look at the stocks listed in that industry. Check out the ETF for the industry and see what companies they are holding.

6. Filtering by sector or industry can be a good start, but you can expand the search even further and filter your list by other details like market cap, dividend yield, or other practical metrics that will help you to decide.

7. Don't waste your energy on trying to catch the absolute bottom of any stock price, nor should you try to stay in a trade until it maxes out at the very top. Keep your focus on growing your net worth and get out when you know it will be to your benefit.

8. Don't give in to FOMO, or the fear of missing out. View each trade as a learning experience and tap into the ones you can and forget about the ones you can't.

9. Choose only one stock to begin with and study the results over time.

10. Use trading charts to give you a clear understanding of the market and stock movements.

11. Follow through with your plan until you get the desired results.

Choosing Stocks That Fit Your Personality

We are naturally drawn to those things that we understand the best. If you are a young twenty-something and have spent your formative years playing lots of video games, you have a quick mind, and know how to stay focused, short-term investing may be the best strategy for you.

On the other hand, if you're nearing retirement age, are slow at making decisions, and like to look at things from all angles, then maybe day trading would be a better choice. If your goal is to generate a little extra income from one month to the next, then dividend trading might be your best option.

Whatever investment style you choose, think it through carefully. It is very important that you understand the stock's volatility, price movements, and expected performance.

Manage Your Risk

Every investment option comes with its own level of risk. Your goal is to preserve your capital and manage that risk with every decision you make. Even if you suffer losses, you want to be sure that you have enough capital left to keep something in play.

Every investment you choose should be an educational experience. Take the time to analyze and calculate the costs, striving to make an informed decision.

Don't Over Complicate It

Keep it as simple as possible. Every stock has its own set of habits and moves; the more you understand these habits — the easier it will be to anticipate how it moves and make decisions accordingly. Once you feel comfortable with one stock, add another, and repeat the process. If you continue this pattern, you are less likely to find yourself in over your head.

What Is an Investment Plan?

Basically, it is a plan of how you will invest in the stock market. It dictates your actions so you don't make impulse decisions that can put your capital at risk. Here is a sample Day Trading plan you can start with until you get your feet wet:

1. Trade one stock at a time
2. When I am familiar with that stock, I will invest in a second one.
3. Trade only within the $20–$40 price range

4. Trade stocks that have an average 30-day volume that ranges a minimum of 1 million shares and a maximum of 2 million
5. The stock should have a medium degree of volatility
6. No trading in biotech stocks
7. I will max my portfolio at five stocks
8. I will study each of the stock's performance during multiple time frames every night
9. I will follow S&P Futures

Here is a sample plan for swing trading

1. Select up to 50 stocks for trade
2. Invest in one at a time
3. When I am comfortable and familiar with one then I will add another
4. The price will be $25 or more
5. Stocks will have an average 30-day volume of 500,000 shares a day or more
6. I will choose 25 for a long watch list

a. Each will have increasing revenues and earnings
b. They will have high relative strength in its leading sectors
c. They will be above the 200 moving average
d. They should be following the S&P Futures

7. I will choose 25 for my short watch list

a. These will have declining revenues and earnings
b. They will have a low relative strength in the leading sectors

c. They will perform below the 200 moving average
d. They should be following the S&P Futures

8. I will study the stochastics signal

The 5 Best Stock Trading Strategies of All Time

Once you've decided on the company to invest in, you're probably eager to get started making money. You need a strategy that dictates just how you want to invest. There are five different strategies for investing in stocks, and it pays to understand a little about each of them to help you determine how you will invest your money.

General Trading: You are anticipating the moves of the overall market, looking for averages that will give you an idea of their direction.

Selective Trading: Selective trading means you will pick out stocks which you expect to perform better than the overall market over the course of the next year.

Buy Low Sell High: Enter the market when the prices are at an extreme low. If you choose well and the stock recovers, you can make a pretty tidy little profit.

Long-Pull Selection: Choose the businesses you expect to prosper over the long-term and will fare better than the average business within their industry.

Bargain Purchases: Choosing stocks that you know are selling below their market value.

Your approach to investing should not be based on impulses but should be thought out rationally, then applied with deliberate discipline. This way, you won't find yourself fretting over every change you see in the market but will be comfortable with your decisions and can understand the movements when they happen.

8 Worst Investing Mistakes to Avoid

When you do things deliberately, you're protecting yourself and your finances. However, new investors often give in to the powerful urge to take a chance on that one risky investment. That and several other mistakes are often at the heart of major financial losses in the market. Learning to avoid these can make a huge difference in how fast you build your portfolio and put you on the right track towards greater profits.

1. ***Investing Before You Understand.*** If you are not well-versed in one industry, you should avoid those stocks. Endeavor to understand the business model and how it plans to increase its profits. Always strive to get a clear picture of where the business is going and how it plans to get there before you commit.

2. ***Allowing Your Love of a Company Overshadow Good Judgment.*** Sometimes we fall in love with a company that is doing very well on the market. Never forget your goal is not to support a company that you love but to make money. While the stock may be doing well, its fundamentals can change at any time, so always keep abreast of what's happening with your stock and events that could impact it. Never love a stock so much that you can't sell it.

3. ***Failing to Exercise Patience.*** It is always wise to exercise patience when investing; the slow, deliberate movement often pays off better than those fast bursts to the top. Your expectations should be realistic so that you're not discouraged when things don't happen quickly.

4. ***Jumping in and Out of Trades too Often.*** While you may make a profit here and there, frequent trades incur frequent fees that will usually eat up any profits you make. Add to that the taxes you will have to pay later, and you could easily end up losing a boatload of money rather than boosting your bottom line.

5. ***Trying to Time the Market.*** Your chances are more likely to meet success from making informed decisions rather than trying to hit the market at a specific time.

6. ***Trying to Get Even.*** If you experience a loss in the market, it is best to walk away rather than wait for an opportunity to regain your money. Holding onto the stock could see you losing even more money as the price continues to slide. It is better to preserve at least some of

your investment by selling your position and reinvesting what's left in a more stable option.

7. **Not Diversifying.** Always invest in more than one industry. This spreads your exposure over a wide range of possibilities and protects your assets. Try to allocate funds to all major sectors and avoid spending more than 10% of your portfolio into one single asset.

8. **Making Emotional Decisions.** Keep a cool head and let your logic govern your decisions. Keep your focus on the long-term results and the averages. It will keep you sane in this business and prevent you from making hasty decisions that could cost you in the long-run.

9. **Create an Action Plan.** Never try to beat the market, but always work towards your personal goals. Be realistic about your expectations and avoid jumping into a stock that makes promises that you know are too good to be true.

10. **Make Your Plan Automatic.** Once you put your plan into action, keep adding to it. Building your investment should continue on throughout your life.

11. **Take Advantage of Your Profits.** There is nothing wrong with skimming a little of your money off the top to enjoy right now, today. Perhaps at the end of the year, you can take 5% of your profits for a little fun. This will give you the incentive to keep pushing forward towards your goals and growing your portfolio.

No doubt, you will make mistakes when you invest in the stock market. Get used to it. It is a major part of investing. However, you can minimize the number of mistakes you make by following these basic guidelines. They will help you to become a better investor over time. By making decisions based on actual facts and data rather than emotions, you will be one step ahead of every other new investor that enters the market.

Chapter 4: Dividend Stocks

How would it feel if you could have a steady stream of income coming in on a regular basis without having to lift a finger to work? Most of us have dreamed about that happening, but some have actually been able to find it through dividend stocks. When you invest in dividend stocks, you are essentially building an ongoing income that will last as long as the company you invest in remains profitable.

However, before you drop all of your money into these stocks, you need to learn just how the dividend system works. How dividends are paid, and the different types of dividends you can choose. You probably enter this arena knowing that dividends are paid on different stocks but understanding how to find and capitalize on cash dividends, stock dividends, and property dividends can make all the difference in how well your investments perform. Here are some basic tips that will help you to enter this type of investment opportunity without making costly mistakes along the way.

When a Company Pays Dividends

Not all companies that earn a profit pay dividends. Some choose to hold onto their profits and then reinvest them back into the business, either by reducing their debt or expanding their operations. Companies that pay out dividends are literally sharing a percentage of their profits with their shareholders. Those who choose to invest in dividend stocks usually have the ultimate goal of using those regular payments to support themselves.

Before a dividend is paid out, it has to first be approved by the company's Board of Directors. If the company pays out monthly, then they have to have approval every month. Once the dividend is approved, there are three dates that an investor needs to know.

Declaration date: the date the company makes a public announcement of its decision to pay a dividend.

Ex-Dividend date: the date the decision is made as to who will be paid. Any shareholders on record on that date will receive a dividend for each share they own.

Payment date: This is the date the dividend is actually distributed to the shareholders. Most dividends are paid out quarterly, but there are several that pay monthly, bi-annually, or annually as well.

Visiting sites like Dividend.com will tell you how often dividends are paid for each stock and how much. For example, if you see a company is paying out $1.00/share every quarter, it means that investors are receiving $.25/share four times a year, not $1 four times a year.

Different Types of Dividends

The most common form of dividend payments is cash dividends. These are paid directly from the profits generated over a period of time. There are several different types of cash dividends. If you own preferred stock, then the company must make those dividend payments preferred shareholders first, before any payments are paid out to common stockholders. Preferred stock dividends are automatically set but common stock dividends can be changed, suspended, or even stopped completely based on the discretion of the Board of Directors.

1. **Property Dividends.** Some companies prefer to give property rather than cash to their shareholders. Property can take any form depending on the holdings of the company. A property dividend could be anything from pencils to gold to cars to salad dressings. These are recorded at market value on the declaration date.

2. **Special Dividends.** Occasionally, a company may choose to make a special dividend for various reasons. These are usually one-time distributions that follow a major success in the business. Perhaps they won major litigation in court, they sold a portion of the business, or they successfully liquidated an investment. These special dividends can be either cash, additional shares in the company or property.

3. **Stock Dividends.** Stock dividends are when an investor receives additional shares in the company rather than a cash distribution. There are a number of reasons why a company may choose to issue shares this way. They may not have enough cash on hand to pay out a cash dividend, or they are trying to dilute the value of the stock to encourage more investors to begin trading. Lowering the price is an excellent enticement to invest. With more shares in the market, the value per share drops. It is a lot easier for investors to pay for a $10 share than one that's $100.

4. *Stock Split.* A stock split is very similar to a stock dividend. A company may opt to double, triple, or quadruple the number of outstanding shares. With a stock split, the value of each share is lowered, but each investor still has the same overall value of his investment. If you owned 100 shares at $100 each and the company offers a 2-1 stock split, you now own 200 shares at $50 each.

Whether or not dividend investing is right for you depends on your goals. When a company decides it is going to pay out dividends, one of the first things it considers is its ability to reinvest the cash it has on hand at a higher rate of interest than the shareholders could. For example, if a company you're investing in is earning 25% on its equity and they have no debt hanging over their head, management could decide to hold all of its earnings confident that the investor will not find another company that is able to bring in that much of a return.

From the investor's perspective, you might be only interested in investing in that company for the dividend to cover your living expenses. These types of investors are not necessarily interested in the actual value of the shares, but in whether or not you're going to be able to pay your bills with the dividends you earn.

The Payout Ratio

The payout ratio is the percentage of net income a company pays out as a dividend. It is important to understand this ratio when choosing which stocks to invest in. This percentage gives you the projected growth of a company and what you can expect from it going forward.

To calculate the payout ratio, look at the company's cash flow statement. For example, if a company's statement says that it paid out

$2.166 billion in dividends to shareholders and its income statement says that it had a net income of $4.347 billion, you could calculate the ratio using the following formula.

$\underline{\$2,166,000,000}$ dividends

$\$4,347,000,000$ net income

The answer 49.8% gives a pretty revealing figure. It shows that the company paid out nearly half of its net profits to shareholders over the year.

The Dividend Yield

Another box you will see when you look up a company's dividend history is the dividend yield. This tells you just how much you are earning in relation to the price of a share of a common stock at the current market price. When you buy a stock that has a high dividend yield, it can generate a nice source of income.

To calculate the dividend yield, divide the annual dividend by the current share price. So, if you were to invest in Starbucks today, your dividend yield would be calculated like this.

$1.44/94.16 = 1.53%

Dividends and Your Taxes

Dividends are taxed at a lower rate than your regular income taxes. Some dividends referred to as "qualified dividends" can be taxed at a higher rate in line with a capital gains tax. To avoid falling into this trap, in order for your dividends earned to be included in that lower rate tax bracket, you must hold the stocks for a minimum of 60 days.

Choosing Stocks That Pay High Dividends

When choosing to invest in dividend stocks, you want to find those that pay the highest of dividends. There are thousands of stocks that pay dividends, so you should be careful to examine each one closely. Look for those companies that have a history of steadily increasing dividends over at least twenty years. Analyze the company's past record until you are confident that they are in a position to continue this trend for the foreseeable future.

Keep in mind that a company's ability to pay dividends is directly related to its cash flow. You are looking for stability. A company can report a net loss and still have a healthy cash flow. If a company is lowering its dividend, you can bet that it's going to lose some stability as investors start to pull out. They will not lower their payout for a problem that they expect to be only temporary. On the other hand, a company that increases its dividend will only do so if the business is capable of maintaining the higher rate for an extended period of time.

DRIPS

As you start to earn dividends, the amount of money you receive may seem miniscule at best, but that's okay. Unless you need a healthy stream of cash flowing in, you can turn around and reinvest that money into buying more stocks through a Dividend Reinvestment Plan (DRIP).

When you enroll in a DRIP plan, you will no longer receive dividend payments, but the money will automatically be used to buy additional shares of the same stock. There are several reasons why you would want to do this:

- The small earnings will automatically be reinvested.
- Most DRIPS plans have minimal or no commission fees
- You are allowed to purchase fractional shares, which over time can increase your wealth significantly.
- You can split your dividend repurchase plan, so you still receive some cash payout while the rest of the money goes to purchase additional shares.

Remember, for every share you purchase, the dividend payout you receive will increase, but with DRIPS, you won't be putting any more of your working capital into the account, and the investment will begin to pay for itself.

Think of how this could work to your benefit. Imagine owning 1,000 shares of a company valued at $49 per share. The annual dividend payout is 1.50/share paid out quarterly. You would receive a quarterly payment of .375 for each share or $375.00. You could receive all of that money each quarter with no problem, but if you don't need the cash to cover living expenses, then you could enroll in DRIPS and reinvest all of it (or some of it) to purchase additional shares of the same stock. $375 could buy you another 7 shares. The next time a dividend payout is due, your income would have moved from $375 to $377.62.

If you continue to repeat this pattern over the next 10 to 20 years, you could see how this would increase your earnings without you ever having to put another dime in the pot. DRIPS is giving yourself a raise.

How to Find the Best Dividend Stocks for Your Portfolio

In order to generate enough of an income from dividends, most people invest in high dividend stocks. When you make good choices and consistently contribute to your portfolio, you can generate quite a passive income that you can live off of during your later years. The most successful investors build up a portfolio based on higher dividend payouts.

There are several ways to find these stocks, but you have to be careful. Often looking at dividend yields can be deceiving, so you need to always be conscious of a possible dividend trap. You need to find those high dividend stocks and still give yourself some type of protection against potential risks where dividends could be cut or eliminated.

- The payout ratio should not exceed 70%, which means that the company is retaining a minimum of 30% of its earning to reinvest.
- Look for companies with a good pricing flexibility. That way, they can raise their prices if the inflation rate becomes too high. This keeps the money flowing into your bank account, even if the economy is not stable.
- Look at the debt-to-equity ratio of the company. It should be 50% or less. This tells you that there is a $1 of net worth to every $1 of debt the company holds.
- The P/E ratio should be 15 or less, which can provide some protection just in case the dividend is cut for some reason.

Do Not Make These 10 Dividend Investing Mistakes

Buying dividend stocks can be tricky. While the potential for profit is great, you can easily fall into huge pitfalls if you're not careful in your search. Don't be hasty in making a decision. Still, with a little knowledge you can avoid many of the mistakes often associated with these kinds of investments.

1.   ***Don't Trust a Hot Tip.*** It doesn't matter how much you trust the person giving it, a tip is only a tip. You can trust someone's sincerity but make it a rule to always verify the information you receive. At the very least, you should look up the company's statements over the last year or two and run the numbers yourself. Look under the hood, kick the tires and so on. Check to see if any insiders are buying shares or if possible, talk directly with someone in the company who may know what's in line for the future.

2.   ***Do the Work.*** Yes, doing the research can be a real pain, but it will pay off in the end. Always do the homework. This will help to keep you from being too emotionally invested in a potential stock. When you understand what you're buying and know how the company is being managed, you're less likely to make an impulse decision that you might regret later. If the market takes a dive, you will know exactly why and already have a back-up plan to cut your losses.

3.   ***Don't Buy/Sell for the Dividend Alone.*** Don't buy the stock just to get the dividend and then sell it right afterward. You'll lose money. Yes, you will collect the dividend as promised, but in most

cases, the price of the share will drop considerably after the payout. At the very best, you can expect to break even. Investors rarely make money on this type of trade, and much of what you earn will be eaten up with fees and commissions.

4. **_Look Beyond the Yield._** Just because a stock has a high yield doesn't always mean that it's not in trouble. Don't be blinded by a high yield to convince you that a stock is worth it. Some companies that have a low yield are far steadier and more reliable than those with a volatile history and a high yield. Always look at the big picture before making a decision. You want to know why the yield is high. Is it because it pays high dividends or because of its low share price?

5. **_Look to the Future._** When you research a stock, you are looking at either its history or where it stands in the present. This is important because it gives you a real time picture of what you can expect from the company. Your goal is to generate a passive income that you can rely on in later years so you also need to know what to expect in the future.

If you are smart, you will look at the company's history to see how well it has performed in the past and use that information to project into the future. If they have historically raised dividends periodically in the past, it might be reasonable to believe they will continue that trend, especially if the numbers look good. Keep a watchful eye out for any news that could have an impact on the company's development or other issues that may not be readily apparent.

6. ***Always Keep a Watch on the Market.*** Don't assume that because you've invested in a company that has a solid history, good numbers, and has hit all of your earmarks, that you should just let everything ride. Even the big stable companies will one day come crashing down. Of the thousands of companies that were on the NYSE 100 years ago, less than two dozen remain. That means that even the massive conglomerates of the past have one day crashed and burned. Always keep a close eye on the market. It's the only way to protect your investment.

7. ***Buying a Stock Based Solely on the Price.*** There is a huge difference between a share price and its actual value. You need to understand this difference. Just because a stock has a low price and appears more affordable doesn't guarantee that it's a good deal. Buying based purely on price is not investing, it is merely gambling, which doesn't yield the kind of results you need to build up a portfolio.

8. ***Keeping a Bad Stock for Too Long.*** When a stock is performing poorly, dump it. That stock is not your friend; it's not someone you owe anything to. If the price is plummeting and there is no indication that it is going to recover anytime soon, waiting to sell is almost a guarantee that you're going to lose. Get rid of it, don't let emotions dictate what you should do; there are thousands of other options that will earn you money. If the stock does recover later on, you can always buy back in.

9. ***Don't Forget Your Taxes.*** Too often, investors get wrapped up in their earnings and fail to account for the debt they owe to Uncle Sam. Anytime you are earning money, there will be taxes to be paid. No matter what investment tool you use, if you're not sure of your tax

obligations, talk to a tax accountant and play it safe. You should do this every year, because tax laws change frequently. You will need to adjust your investment plan to ensure that your earnings are more than enough to keep the IRS at bay.

10.   ***Taking the Media Too Seriously.*** When you start to research different stocks there will be an endless stream of media reports, financial analysts, and opinions about what is a good or a bad stock. Many of them have very good information to consider but they are not always right. The value of their information is only as good as their resources. No source is 100% reliable. Always do your best to verify any information you receive, especially if you are not getting it directly from the company itself.

Choosing the best high dividend stocks is not rocket science, but it can make you feel like you're navigating one the craters on the moon. There are so many dark areas where you can get into trouble, you will have to be extra careful not to fall into any of the traps that catch so many novice investors.

What You Need to Know About Dividend Tax Rates

As your profits start to roll in, it is important to keep everything in perspective. As much as you'd like to think so, all of that money is not yours. As usual, Uncle Sam is sitting on the sideline waiting for his share. Once you start collecting dividends, you'll have to set some of those proceeds aside to keep him appeased.

Most dividends are paid in the form of cash but depending on where you decide to put your investments, you may also receive them in the form of additional stocks, stock options, property, services, or options. No matter what instrument you invest in, it is considered profit, and you must claim it on your income taxes.

Ordinary vs. Qualified Dividends

There are two different types of dividends you might be receiving. Ordinary dividends are those received from the profits of a company. The amount you receive is usually based on the type of stock you have. Preferred stocks pay more than the common stock investments, but any dividend received from a preferred stock will still be considered an ordinary dividend unless it is stipulated otherwise.

Qualified dividends meet the IRS's requirements for capital gains taxes, which are taxed at a higher rate than ordinary dividends. Depending on your tax bracket, you could expect to pay anywhere from nothing to as much as 20% of your income.

Under the current tax laws, you must report all dividend income received even if it is only a small amount. If you received more than $10 from any one company, you will need to file a Form 1099-DIV declaring the exact amount you received. If the dividends you received come from a trust, estate or an S-corporation, you should also file a Schedule K-1, which will determine the percentage of dividends that you must pay taxes on.

You should automatically receive the required forms you should file from the company, but if for some reason you don't, you are still required to report the income on your tax return. Even if you don't receive an actual payout of those dividends, the IRS still sees them as taxable income. So, even if you reinvest them into purchasing more stocks, you are still required to report that as income.

How to Report Dividends

You can report your dividend income on your regular 1040 From. If your total income received amounts to more than $1,500 or if some of the dividends you receive are as a nominee for someone else, then you must also file a Schedule B form.

The thrill of seeing your money working for you can be truly amazing, but to ensure that those successes you receive are not dampened by trouble with the IRS, always take the time to file your income properly. This way, you can really enjoy the money you earn without reservation.

Chapter 5: Day Trading

If dividend investing is a little too slow for you, a faster way to get generate new cash is with day trading.

What Is Day Trading?

Day trading works the same as regular stock market investing, but all of your transactions are completed within one trading day. In essence, you buy and sell before the close of the trading day. Traders who make these types of trades are considered to be speculators, a form of trading that carries much higher risks.

One of the reasons for closing during a single day is to protect the gains investors might have received throughout the course of the trading day. Once the market closes, events can happen that could reverse the trend and they would be unable to manage things. A drop in prices can easily occur after the close of one day and before the open of the next and with that drop, much of their profits could go with it. However, by selling your position before the close of the day, you lock in whatever profits you have earned and thus cut your risks.

Day trades can be made in any market but are most commonly transacted in the stock or the foreign trade markets. Investors rely heavily on leverage for these short-term trading strategies, focusing on making their money on seemingly insignificant price movements.

As a day trader, you will need to keep abreast of any news events that may have an impact on the trades you're making. This strategy is called "trading the news" where you respond to economic statistics, interest rate movements, or corporate earnings. These types of events are subject to market psychology, and investors will react with quick but significant moves. Day traders anticipate these movements and take advantage of them to capitalize on their earnings.

While the risk can be very high, the attraction of day trading is the potential for amazingly fast and impressive profits. To get those though, you need to be a fast decision-maker, disciplined, and diligent enough to do the required research to improve your chances of success.

There are many reasons why you might want to try your hand at day trading.

- You can profit when the price is rising and when it is falling
- You get additional margin and can use the leverage and the quick movements in the market to capitalize on gains.
- While research is necessary, detailed research into a company's fundamentals is not necessary. You are tapping into small fluctuations so you don't need long-term investment strategies.
- You earn cash fast.

These are just some of the advantages of entering into day trading. If you think you have the fortitude and are a fast thinker, then the next step is to just pick a stock and start trading.

How to Start Day Trading

Day trading sounds simple enough, but there is definitely a learning curve. Picking the best stocks to trade is only the beginning. The most successful traders have become very skilled at applying what they call the "The Rule of the Three P's," Planning, Practice, and Patience.

Planning. You will definitely need a trading plan to get started. Develop a personal map to help you navigate your trades. You are entering a highly volatile market and things will be moving quickly. If you're not prepared, you'll miss your marks and end up losing more money than you'll gain.

Practice. You won't get it right the first time out of the gate. It might be best to practice with one of the online trading platforms that let you test out your theories before you actually put money in the game. The more practice you get, the better you'll be at predicting when many of these volatile movements will happen. If you don't get it right, don't let that discourage you. Some of the most experienced day traders miss out from time to time. Just keep trying until you hit your rhythm.

Patience. Once you have a good trading plan and you get started, you'll experience some ups and downs. You need patience enough to stick to your plan to the end.

A day trader knows the when, what, and how to trade every stock before he enters the market. To do that, you need to understand how to use volatility to your advantage.

Volatility is directly linked to the activity of short-term traders and reflects the dispersion of a stock's returns on the market index. It can be determined by the difference between a stock's high and lows for a given day and then divided by the actual price for the same day. But the fluctuation of the price is only one factor that measures volatility. For example, a stock with a $50 share price that fluctuates as much as $5 in a single day is considered to be a lot more volatile than a $150 share that also fluctuates in the $5 range. It is the percentage of the move that also factors into its volatility.

The best day traders look to trade the most volatile stocks. It is the most efficient means of making money fast. These stocks tend to offer the best profit potential, but they come with their own level of risk. If you're aiming to try your hand at one of these, you need two things:

1. Where to find the most volatile stocks to trade
2. How to trade them with technical indicators

The best way to find a volatile stock is to run a stock screen through a platform like stockfetcher.com. These sites use filters to track the most active stocks. For example, you can select stocks that average moves of 5% or greater between opening and closing on each of the last 100 days. You can also filter by stock prices as well.

For a more intensive search, another platform you can use is Finviz.com. Its free version will give you a list of the top gainers and the top losers in the market each day. You also have the option to filter the results further, looking for details on market capitalization, volume, and performance. You can be very specific in the type of filters you use so that you can end up with a list of stocks that meet very exacting parameters.

Nasdaq.com also lists the markets biggest gainers and loser, but their results are not filtered for volatility. Instead, you'll get a list of stocks that have the potential of being volatile. You'll need to manually sift through the list to see which stocks have the possibility of going volatile on a trading day.

Now to the question of how to trade them. When you have chosen your stock and are ready to make a trade, you need to be patient and wait for the precise moment to enter the market. One of the biggest advantages you will have is something called "directional bias." This is when specific indicators will be observed that tell you in which way the price is moving. You must always watch the price action to determine if the price is swinging high or low in comparison to previous waves.

The Stochastic Oscillator. Another useful tool you can use is the stochastic oscillator for predicting volatile stocks. This filters for stocks that may not have a very clear trend. Even when a stock is volatile, it can fall into a range before taking off in either direction. Just one single move can quickly change things, so the best thing to do is to hold off until you get confirmation that a price is going to reverse in one way or another.

In such cases, the price may not have a clear-cut direction, but may simply be moving sideways for a time. The best investment strategy is to wait until the price moves above 80 and then falls again. That's when you sell close to or at the top of its range. You can place your stop directly above the new high and your target at 75% of the total range. So, if the range has a high of $1, place your target at $0.25 over the low.

At the bottom, you can establish a long position if the stochastic falls below 20 and begins to rally above it. Place your stop underneath the new low and your target should go 75% up from the bottom. Again, if the range has a high of $1, the target can be at $0.25 below the high.

With the stochastic oscillator, make your trades when they hit 80 and above for uptrends and 20 or below when they are in a downtrend. You will have to move quickly though. If it is truly in a trend, even a delay of one minute could move the price too far away from your target to make any worthwhile trade.

When you are in a trade, ignore signals that may say contrary to what you believe. Let the trade play through. It will either hit the target or the stop.

Volatile stocks are a great way to earn fast money if you have the stomach for it. If you can successfully identify a trend, you will have access to even greater profits. Just follow the directional bias in order to help you make your decision.

Keep in mind that just because a stock is volatile, doesn't necessarily mean that it will trend. Prices can move back and forth sideways for long periods of time. When you see that stochastic reaches either the 80 or 20 mark and then pulls back, it is an indication of a good opportunity to enter the trade.

Day Trading Strategies

There are no hard and fast secrets to successful day trading. While it can be extremely lucrative, it is full of potholes that could cost you just as much, if not more money than you can make. The secret is to develop a well-thought-out plan that you can follow to the letter. The problem with this is that most newbies do not fully understand the game, nor do they have any idea how to create such a plan. Here are just a few tips that can help you develop a good day trading plan to launch you into the market.

1. ***Never Stop Learning.*** The more knowledge you have, the less likely you will make a costly mistake. When you day trade, you need to be aware of all of the latest news in the market. You want to know anything that could happen that might have an impact on the stocks you're investing in. Never shrink back from doing the extra work, it will pay off in the end. This is even more important when the news is directly related to stocks, you're planning on investing in.

2. ***Have an Investment Fund Ready.*** Know exactly how much money you are willing and able to put at risk for every trade you plan to make. On average, day traders usually put up approximately 1-2% of their portfolio into day trades. Some only a half percent. Once you know that amount, portion it out to the stocks you're willing to invest in, but know that there is always a risk, so never put up more than you can lose.

3. ***Make Sure You Have Time.*** Day trading takes time. Because you will have to constantly be watching the movements of the market, it could consume an entire day. If you don't have the time to dedicate to the process, it is better for you to find other ways to invest your money.

4. ***Start Small.*** Don't try to tackle too many stocks at once. When you're beginning, you need to get the feel for the market. Start with only one stock and when you gain your confidence increase it to two. Some even start smaller than that with buying fractional shares rather than a whole single share. Some brokers like Stockpile, will allow you to buy a small percentage of a share, so you can invest in higher-priced stocks without putting a whole lot of money at risk.

5.   ***Stay Away From Penny Stocks.*** The tendency for newcomers is to look at the cheapest stocks on the market. Penny stocks are those stocks that are usually priced at $5 or less per share. On the surface, this looks like a great stock to start with, but penny stocks are questionable at best. The chances of getting a windfall from them is minimal. Most stocks that are trading below $5 a share have often fallen to the Penny Stock list because they have been delisted from the major stock exchanges and are already in trouble. Unless you see very clear signs of a reversal, your best bet is to stay clear of these seemingly good bargains.

6.   ***Timing is Everything.*** Learn the timing of the market so you know when it's time to jump in. For example, many investors may place an order overnight for the next business day. This means that as soon as the market opens, those orders will be executed so you will see a lot of movement during the first hours of trading, but that is not always a clear picture of market movement. It might be best to wait an extra half an hour until all those orders settle down Usually, the middle of the day is the less volatile with activity increasing the closer you get to the closing bell.

7.   ***Take Advantage of Limit Orders.*** Market orders are placed at the best price offered at that specific time. They are not necessarily the best price for you. Limit orders, however, guarantee that the order will only be fulfilled at the price you set. If the price you set is not available, the order will not be filled. Limit orders give you the opportunity to place an order and know exactly the price you will pay.

8.   ***Be Realistic.*** No one will win all of the time, but that doesn't mean you can't turn a profit. Your goal is to make more money than

you lose. If you keep your limits within a set percentage of your account and plan your entry and exits accordingly, then you have a good chance of gaining more profits than losses, but you will have to stick to your plan and follow through on it.

9.   ***Never Lose Your Cool.*** There will be those days when you won't have any idea what the market is doing. On those days, keep your emotions at bay. Always make decisions based on clear logic and reasoning, even if the market is not making any sense at the moment.

10.   ***Never Stray From Your Plan.*** When you are day trading, decisions have to be made fast. That can be very difficult if you haven't done your homework. The price could catapult completely out of your reach while you're trying to figure things out. That's why it's so important to do your homework before you enter the market, so you know the exact point to enter and exit. Creating a plan beforehand and relying on it as a guide is the secret to successful day trade. No matter what the numbers say, don't allow them to lure you into chasing profits but make sure that you follow the day trader's mantra – *Plan your trade and trade your plan.*

Making a Decision

Now that you have made a list of those stocks that are potential winners, you now have to decide which one to buy. A day trader usually looks at three factors:

- **Liquidity.** When a stock is liquid, you have room to enter and exit at a good price. Look for tight spreads between the bid and the asking price, or a low slippage price. The difference between what one would expect to pay for a stock and its actual price.

- **Volatility.** the expected price range within a single trading day. The more volatile the price the greater the chance for profits (or losses).

- **Volume.** How many times a particular stock has been bought and sold within a set time period. When you see a volume increase in a stock, there is heightened interest, and you can expect some type of price jump.

Once you've decided what stocks to buy and your plan is set on when to enter the market, you need to decide when to sell. Ideally, you want to sell when the price hits your target, but that is not the only time you can exit.

- Scalping: selling as soon as you make a profit.
- Fading: selling after the price has made a rapid move upward.
- Pivots: selling at the highest price point of the day
- Momentum: selling after news releases or trending moves.

If you find that the interest in the stock is beginning to diminish, you should not hesitate to sell. You should give the same attention to exiting your trade as you do for entering it. Remember, it must be specific enough that you know when to execute it without much deliberating.

Charts

Another way you can determine when to enter the market is by reading chart patterns. Candlestick patterns can take up a whole book on their own. They provide a wealth of ways to look for an entry point. However, one of the most common is the doji reversal pattern.

1. Find a volume spike, which shows if traders are supporting this price level.
2. Find the support for that price. It could be the low or the high of the previous day.
3. Find the level 2 situation, which shows all open orders for that stock.

By following these basic steps, you should be able to anticipate when a price will turn around and offer more favorable positions.

Stop-Loss Orders

Stop-loss orders are meant to manage your losses. The order can be placed either in a low position or above a recent high to automatically sell when the price reaches that point. Using this will protect you from losing everything if the trade doesn't go your way.

Day trading is tricky at best. It is not something that you can get into blindly and expect to win. It takes skill, insight, and discipline. In time, with enough practice and determination, there is a very good chance that you will be successful.

Chapter 6: Real Estate Investing

Real estate opens a wealth of opportunities that one can parlay into a great fortune with the right tools. Unlike investing in the stock market, the principles behind real estate are pretty straightforward. But that doesn't mean that it will be easy breezy when you try to put them into action.

There are three ways you can make money from real estate.

- Increasing property value
- Rentals
- Investing in businesses that depend on real estate

In fact, the three options listed above are the most common ways to generate a nice passive income from the property you own. By learning just a few basic strategies to implement these, you could be well on your way to financial freedom.

Increasing Your Property Value

No matter what you do with your property, outside influences can still have a negative impact on its worth. Every decade or so, there seem to be occasions when the rate of inflation is expected to extend beyond the rate of long-term debt at the time. When that happens, you will find more people willing to extend themselves by borrowing money to finance a major property purchase. Then they sit back and wait for the inflation rate to go back up again. When it does, they can pay off their mortgage with a lower dollar value.

The key is to time the market just right. You need to know how to look at a project, analyze its price and timing, and decide if you will be able to create a good income that will be sufficient enough to support a higher valuation than what is currently evident.

Making Money From Rental Property

While rental property is not always as passive as it might seem, collecting rent is so simple anyone can do it. If you own any kind of property, you can simply rent it out to anyone who wishes to use it. It doesn't even matter what type of property it is; it could be a house, an apartment, or farmland. The money you get from their use of it can be quite lucrative.

As the owner of the property, it will be your responsibility to make sure that the property is being maintained in a usable condition. That means that you will have to be ever vigilant in repairs, supervision, and handling the negative aspects of undesirable tenants. You'll have to be insured against theft or other hazards and be proactive about possible concerns that may come up in relation to your property.

The good news though is that if you are a savvy property owner, there are ways to manage all of those things and still make a tidy profit. There are tools that have been designed that can make property management much easier than it has been in years. One you will find very practical is a special financial ratio, the capitalization rate. To understand this rate and how it works, consider this situation.

If you own a property that is earning $100,00/year and its price is set at $1,000,000, you could apply this formula by dividing the earnings by the value of the house to get the capitalization rate.

$100,000 / $1,000,000 = 0.1$ or 10%

You could immediately earn 10% on your investment if you chose to pay cash for the purchase.

You can think of this in the same way you think of stocks. The worth of any real estate property is based on the net present value of the cash it generates for the owner and the cash flow it generates in relation to the price paid for its purchase. In essence, rental income can become a hedge to protect you during economic and financial collapses.

Of course, not all real estate is the same; some will be better suited for generating rental income while others are not. When you make a purchase at the right price but also at the right time, and you can find the right tenant to fill the space, you need not fear any upcoming real estate collapse. You will be collecting a steady stream of rental checks that will carry you through. However, if you don't plan the whole thing right, you could find yourself collecting rents that are far below the market and be stuck in that drain until the market recovers.

Investing in Businesses That Depend on Real Estate

There are lots of businesses that rely heavily on real estate. Many of them, like hotels, provide special services to the public. Other property owners provide office space for businesses, and there are those that can take an empty field and provide useful parking garages for those who drive to the area. Car washes, vending machines, agriculture, and more, the list is endless.

The trick for entering this highly lucrative market is to learn just enough to get started, but not so much that you become overwhelmed.

Most new investors learn through a trial-and-error process. In this process, they usually make costly mistakes that can lead them to regrets. However, a plan that will help you to avoid such missteps and get you on the path to passive income can save you a world of time and frustration.

Start Investing One Step at a Time

The steps listed below will help you to make your first initial steps in the real estate market. After you are confident you can carry them out, use them as a checklist to make sure that you don't miss anything crucial that could cost you later on.

Identify Where You Are Financially

Real estate is probably the fastest way to reach financial independence. It is usually the goal that everyone strives to reach. It is one of the best ways to generate enough income to support you financially. But to get to that point, you have to be in a good financial position; you need enough savings to start the ball rolling.

If after looking at your financial situation, you're not quite there yet, there are things you can do to get you there faster.

There are five fundamental stages of wealth:

Stage 1: Survival state – where you are just making enough money to get by. This is the stage where you begin to pay off your debts and get relief from your financial burdens.

Stage 2: Stability state – your finances are not getting worse and you're managing to get your bills paid, and what little you have left you can start saving.

Stage 3: Saver state – you can pay all your bills and have a little bit left over to build up a nice little nest egg.

Stage 4: Growth state – At this point, your savings is turning into a tidy sum that you can seriously consider investing. Your savings should now be generating enough interest that it's worth noticing. If you're reinvesting those earnings, you are starting to get your money to work for you.

Stage 5: Income – you are now in a position where the money you have set aside can generate income for you.

It is important to understand your financial position. Some real estate strategies we discuss later on will be more appropriate for certain stages than others.

Choose Your Investment Strategy

While real estate investing is pretty simple, you still need a business plan. It doesn't have to be detailed, but you need to have a clear idea of what you're going to do. Choose one single strategy that will help you move from the stage you are starting with to the next level. Make sure you build some flexibility into your plan so that you're not derailed by unexpected events. Here are just a few ideas to get your started.

- Lease a large home and sublet rooms to tenants to cover your expenses
- Offer to find good deals for other real estate investors for a fee
- Help buyers find property to invest in, learning the ins and outs of real estate in the process.
- Help landlords find good tenants for their empty spaces
- Become a building manager/superintendent for other real estate investors

These strategies work well for those who are in either the **survival or stability state**. Any of these strategies will allow you to generate extra income without having to shell out a large sum of cash in the process. At the same time, you'll learn everything about the industry without having to spend any extra time taking classes or studying up on the latest policies. It'll be like getting paid to learn.

Start Cutting Back on Your Expenses

If you're at the **saver** stage, then you can do all of the things in the previous stages, but you can also add a few more steps to the process. For one thing, you should start cutting down on your household expenses.

- Use the additional income to pay down your mortgage so you can eliminate your monthly payment.

- Flip your house while you live in it. When you sell it, you create tax-free savings that you can use to invest in other properties.

- Purchase a house that needs significant repairs, move-in while fixing it and then rent it out at a higher price later.

- Become a real estate wholesaler, which is basically collecting a finder's fee for matching the deal with the right investor. This works great for those who may be interested in flipping a house in poor condition or plans to use it for some other profitable purchase. Homeowners who are in jeopardy of foreclosure are more likely to be favorable to such a deal because it allows them to get out from under without having to lose everything.

If you are at the **growth** stage, you are ready to grow your net worth into something much bigger. This is the perfect stage for jumping into real estate. There are several ways you can do this:

- Flipping houses: this allows you to generate larger sums of cash to reinvest in other profits.

- Use your savings to pay all cash for property.

- Borrow from several different properties you already own and then pay them down quickly one at a time.

- Buy three properties but sell or rent two. The money from the rental can pay for your living expenses on the third.

- Do a property exchange. Under the IRS's tax-free property exchange you can use Form 1031 to put off paying taxes on any property you sell if you can replace it with a similar piece of property. It makes it possible for you to start small and then grow your portfolio without having to face the negative impact of paying federal taxes with each property you purchase. The process would look like this:

  o You need enough cash on hand for a down payment and closing costs
  o Buy a basic rental property
  o Rent the property and save a portion of the rental for a few years
  o Sell the property
  o Use the 1031 form to purchase another, larger property at a discount
  o Repeat

Use Your Retirement Account to Purchase Rental Property

By using your tax-free retirement accounts to invest in real estate, you can garner a lot more income to invest, and avoid paying hefty income taxes for your purchase. Self-directed accounts like IRAs, ROTH IRAs, 401Ks allow you to invest those funds in real estate and defer the income taxes you would have otherwise paid.

Maximize Your Income by Utilizing Existing Equity in Your Investments

If you're already at the income stage, you can maximize the income you're generating by selling low-quality properties and buying better ones. You could refinance any of your existing debt and exchange it for fixed low-interest loans and save even more money.

These are just some suggestions for real estate investment strategies. Probably one of them will be more appealing to you than others. Perhaps you have ideas of your own that you would like to consider. The main point is that you have to start with a viable and workable plan to make a success in real estate.

How to Select a Target Market

Your next step would be to pick a target market. Whatever market you choose will have a direct impact on the kind of cash you can generate. Most people prefer to choose a market that is close to their home. It is more efficient and less stressful than investing in properties that are out of your physical reach.

This does not mean that you can't invest in properties far away; it is definitely possible, but you do need to weigh the costs. Whatever market you choose, you need to evaluate the potential carefully.

You also need to do a good market analysis of the area you're interested in. Study the region for employment opportunities, rent prices, and potential population growth. Check the area for the following:

- Is the area convenient?
- Walkability
- Crime
- Schools
- Public transportation
- Local laws
- Taxes
- HOAs
- Etc.

With the above criteria, you can determine if you will be able to work with your target market or if you need to find another location. Start your examination with the larger metropolitan area and then gradually narrow the research down to smaller areas to determine the best location.

1. *Identify Your Criteria for Investment Property*

Determine what you think is a good investment. Write yourself an investment profile that you can show to others. This could be used to generate possible leads to properties you may want to pursue. This list could include property locations, prices, or a specific niche.

Your profile should also have a projection for how much rent you can charge for a property. You might want to start with a basic property to get your feet wet. Choose something you can live in for the moment and then grow from there.

You can find the best land, the most perfect home, at the ideal price, but if it's in a poor location, you may not be able to resell/rent it or if you do, you may not be able to get much of a profit from it.

When you find what you're looking for, even if everything appears to be right, do a little research and check nearby listings in the area. You'll get a pretty good picture of what similar properties are selling for so you can make accurate projections about your potential profits.

Even if you know you're buying a fixer-upper, it is important to have the property inspected. Don't hesitate to ask questions. You need to know how much you're going to need to put into the property and still be able to turn a profit.

Finally, make sure that there is a good chance of turning a profit before you take action. Don't forget to calculate the mortgage rate, utilities, taxes, insurance, repairs, and upkeep. All of that will have a bearing on how successful you'll be with your first investment.

No matter what you do, if the deal doesn't feel right, don't be afraid to walk away. Holding out for the best deals is going to be one of your best secrets to success.

2. Get Your Support System in Place

Real estate is best enjoyed with others. While you may be the sole investor on a project, you will still need a team of experts to turn to. Contractors, designers, real estate agents, and advisors could just be the beginning of your list. A good team could be ready to pick up the slack when you get into an area where you lack knowledge and expertise.

3. Set Up Your Financing Options

Depending on your credit rating and your financial situation, your options can vary. Here are just a few resources you can tap into.

- Federal Housing Administration
- Veterans Administration
- Conforming Loans (Fannie Mae/Freddie Mac)
- Bank Loans
- Hard Money Loans
- Private Lenders
- Seller Financing

It can be tricky to choose the right lender, but this is where you can call on the advice from your team.

4. Get Your Down Payment and Closing Costs Ready

While you can launch your new business with other people's money, you need to have some money of your own to invest. In most cases, a down payment is required to even get the ball rolling. Some down payments can be as little as 3% of the purchase price. Closing costs can also vary. Even in the best of deals, you may need as much as $20,000 of your own cash on hand.

5. Start Looking for Deals

Finding the right property requires a lot of legwork. Good deals will not just mysteriously find their way to you, you're going to have to start looking under every rock and peering into every nook and cranny before you find the property that you know is right.

Your marketing budget can be launched with practically nothing, but if you have some money to put towards it, the process gets a lot easier. Here are just a few ideas that have proven to be effective marketing campaigns.

o   ***Free campaign:*** Find an agent who will agree to send you leads based on your list of expectations.

o   ***Referrals and Networking:*** For a little extra money, you can have business cards or flyers printed with your requirements so that people can contact you when they find something.

o   ***Do a Drive or Walk By:*** Make it a habit to visit your target neighborhood looking for possible deals. For Sale by Owner signs can be quite promising, but you can also look for homes that have been vacant for a long time, appear to be in need of repair, or even have for rent signs posted.

o   ***Wholesalers:*** Let real estate wholesalers find the deals for you. Contact a few of them and get their list of possible properties.

If you have a little extra money to spend:

o **Start a Direct Mail Campaign:** Create your own letters or postcards to send to property owners in your target market. You can find the names and addresses by paying a list company. Some of these lists can be very lucrative:

- Absentee owner properties
- Multi-unit property owners
- Owner-occupied homes
- Recent evictions
- Delinquent property taxes
- Expired real estate listings
- Pre-foreclosure and foreclosure properties
- Estate and probate sales

o **Use your online presence:** Utilize social media. Set up a dedicated page to your real estate marketing plans on sites like Facebook, LinkedIn, Twitter, etc. Create an online business card to let people know what you're looking for.

o **Car/Yard Signs:** Invest in magnetic or vinyl signs for your car or yard.

o **Advertising:** Online or print advertising can get to areas that are difficult for you to reach on your own. Use resources like Google Adwords and don't neglect marketing in local newspapers, magazines, and radio. These efforts are a little pricey, but with the right strategy, they can get you good results fast.

6. Make a Schedule

You will need to set aside time to dedicate to your real estate venture. Be realistic with how much time you have to spend. Set your priorities first and then commit to the schedule you've set.

10 Important Features of Profitable Real Estate

To ensure that the property you choose is going to be profitable, it must have certain features. Even if it is a wreck and appears to be ready for demolition, there are still certain things you need to be sure of before your investment will be worthwhile. Here are the 10 most important features any property should have.

A Good Neighborhood

A look at the neighborhood can tell you a lot about the type of tenants you will attract. A location near a university will attract a lot of students. A location outside of the urban area may attract more families with children.

Property Taxes

All properties have taxes that need to be paid. You need to know how much they are and if the owners owe any back taxes. You can find out everything you need to know about the taxes with a visit to the county or city assessment office.

School System

If you are going to rent to families, you'll need to know something about the schools in the community. Few families are willing to buy or rent a home in a community with substandard schools.

Crime

Check with the local police department or visit the local library to see the latest crime statistics for the neighborhood. Pay extra attention to figures related to petty crimes, vandalism, and serious offenders.

Job Opportunities

Your best bet is to find properties in communities that are expanding their job market. These are more likely to attract buyers and renters to the area. Find out about job availabilities with the US Bureau of Labor Statistics. It can be a huge plus if major corporations are moving to the area. This kind of news often results in property values increasing as more people will be needed to fill those new jobs.

Neighborhood Amenities

What does the neighborhood have to offer? For children, there should be parks, playgrounds, movie theaters, etc. For adults, there should be fitness centers, public transportation, restaurants, and other entertainment venues.

Prospects for the Future

The city planning department should have information on any new developments that are proposed for the area. A lot of construction is a pretty good sign that the future is promising. However, be on the lookout for how those developments would impact property values.

Vacancies

When there are a lot of houses for rent or an excessive number of properties listed for sale, it could be a sign that the area is in a decline. Often when neighborhoods go into decline, property owners are forced to lower rents to keep their units occupied. On the other hand, when there are only a few vacancies in the area, you can comfortably ask for more rent.

Average Rent

If you're planning on renting, then you need to know just how much you can expect to get for a property in the area. You want to make sure that the rent will be enough to cover mortgage payments, property taxes, maintenance, and other forms of upkeep. Project these numbers into the future because what may be affordable today, could be marked out of your reach in five years, which may leave you forced to sell in an unfavorable market or go into bankruptcy later.

Exposure to Natural Disasters

It's not something that most people want to think about, but exposure to natural disasters can negatively impact your potential returns. Whether your home is in a flood zone, hurricane region, or earthquake-prone area, it's going to cost you either in insurance claims or direct repairs.

The best place to get reliable information is through government agencies, but don't stop there. The people in the community usually know everything about what's happening in the neighborhood. Talk to renters and property owners alike. Renters are more likely to give you a better picture since they have nothing to lose. They will tell you about any negatives you may not have thought of, but property owners will have a completely different perspective. If you keep these features in mind and your expectations realistic, you'll know when you've found the right property.

Top 15 Real Estate Investing Strategies

The strategies listed below are meant to give you an idea of the various ways you can generate your own income.

- **Flipping Houses:** Finding properties that need improvement, upgrading, or renovating and then reselling them at a profit.

- **Wholesaling:** Finding good deals on properties and then reselling them to a third party for an additional fee.

- **House Hacking:** Buy a multi-unit property and rent out the additional units. For example, buying a house and renting out the basement, or buying a duplex and renting out the extra unit.

- **BRRRR Investing:** Buy-Remodel-Rent-Refinance-Repeat. Buy a fixer-upper below market value, finance the property and then renovate. Refinance with a long-term mortgage and then take out your initial capital for a new investment.

- **The Cash Rental Strategy:** Buying property in cash. When you have completed the renovations and rented it out, you keep the majority of the money collected for yourself and can quickly invest in another property.

- **The Trade-Up Plan:** Using the IRS 1031 tax-free exchange to progressively trade up to bigger and better properties.

- **Hard Money Lending:** Giving short-term loans to investors who plan to fix-and-flip properties. Loans like these are usually given with high interest rates and up-front fees, so you'll make a good amount of cash in a short time.

- **Discounted Note Investing:** Buying real estate debt at a discount.

- **Syndications & Crowdfunding:** Pooling your money with individual investors to buy the perfect piece of property.

- **REITs:** Investing in companies that manage real estate. REIT stands for real estate investment trusts. You can buy REITs on the stock market, allowing you to own a small part of commercial real estate businesses and earn dividends on the profits in the interim.

Real estate can be a pretty lucrative business, but you have to be smart about it. There are many ways to achieve financial freedom through real estate, and each one has its own pros and cons. You can pick a strategy that works best for you or do several at a time. If one doesn't work right for you, then try another until you hit on your perfect match.

Chapter 7: Other Ways to Grow Wealth

The path to financial freedom can take you in many directions. Investing in the stock market and real estate are the most well-known entry points for new investors. They offer the lowest amount of risk in the investment world and give you a much better chance of success in the global marketplace.

That said, once you've gotten your feet wet and have acquired a taste for collecting passive money, you may want to start investing in other instruments that could prove to be even more lucrative for the private investor.

How to Start Investing in Exchange-Traded Funds (ETFs)

You've probably heard the term ETF mentioned in financial reports on the news and may not be sure of what it really is. You know it has something to do with the stock market, but you're not exactly sure about what they do.

ETFs or Exchange Traded Funds are groups of various investments that have been collected together to form one unit. These funds can be purchased on an exchange just like stocks with similar price movements.

Inside an ETF, you will find many different assets as opposed to a stock that will only be representative of only one asset. Because one share in an ETF covers so many assets, they are one of the easiest ways to diversify your portfolio. One ETF could possibly hold thousands of different stocks spread across several different industries.

Depending on the industries you may be interested in, you can purchase different types of ETFs.

- Bond ETFs consist of government, corporate, state, and municipal bonds.
- Industry ETFs can be compiled from stocks in a specific industry like banking, agriculture, or technology.
- Commodity ETFs would be a collection of different commodities like gold or oil.
- Currency ETFs include a selection of foreign currencies
- Inverse ETFs use the strategy of shorting various stocks. Shorting is the strategy of selling at a higher price and then repurchasing them after the price drops.

The only one on the list, the inverse ETFs are technically not exchange traded funds, but are actually exchange-traded notes or ETNs. These are bonds that are traded on the market like a stock and are banked by a bank.

Buying and selling ETFs

You can purchase ETFs through a broker. You have your choice of using either a traditional broker-dealer or an online broker. You can also use a robo-advisor, an automated investment system that uses certain algorithms to help you to build up your portfolio.

Advantages of ETFs

As an investor, you can buy or sell a wide range of these securities with one single transaction. This also saves you on commission fees as well. You might even find some brokers who offer no-commission trading on ETFs, cutting your costs even more.

Aside from saving on commissions, there are other ways ETFs can save you money. They cost very little to operate and manage. Because they are tracking an index, it is more passively-managed requiring far less time to govern, and since they are widely diversified, their level of risk is much lower.

Disadvantages of ETFs

There are some ETFs that have higher fees. These are the ones that are generally focused on one single industry, so your diversification is extremely limited. There are also some ETFs that are actively managed by portfolio managers that do all of the buying and selling. These come with higher fees in order to pay the manager's fees for overseeing the fund's movements.

Indexed-Stocks ETFs

These funds provide investors the option to sell short, buy on margin, and acquire as little as one single share. If you choose to invest in Indexed-Stock ETFs, be watchful of those that might be heavily concentrated on one single industry or a limited number of stocks.

Dividends: Most ETFs pay dividends in proportion to their investment. As a result, you can expect to receive periodic payments for the earnings from the different securities for as long as you hold the fund. If for some reason, the fund is liquidated, you will receive your portion of its residual value.

Taxes

You'll also get to save, as these instruments are more tax-efficient that mutual funds. Because all trading happens through an exchange, there is no need to physically redeem the shares every time a transaction is completed. Since redeeming shares can trigger tax liabilities, conducting all transactions on the exchange keeps you from getting hit with taxes every time a transaction occurs.

Market Impact

Because of the increasing popularity of ETFs, more funds are now being created. This may not be good news for some investors since it means lower trading volumes for many of them. As more funds enter the market, it may become more difficult to buy and sell at such low volumes, which could leave you trapped in an instrument with no way out.

If you choose to invest in ETFs, make sure you select one that can help you to achieve your goals. You should feel confident that the fund you choose will give you the kind of exposure you need to grow your profits. Make sure that you're making your decision based on what works for you and not what others expect.

Start Making Money Now with Peer-to-Peer Lending

Another way to grow your wealth and gain financial freedom is with peer-to-peer lending. In the past, the only way to get a loan for a major purchase was through a financial institution. Now, you can become your own lending institution and collect interest on the money you loan to others. The majority of peer-to-peer loans are used for personal reasons like consolidating debt or home improvements.

How it works

Making a loan with peer-to-peer lending is very different from how they are made with financial institutions. With a traditional loan, the bank will finance the loan with funds deposited from other customers. In contrast, peer-to-peer lending involves matching borrowers and investors through an online lending platform. As an investor, you decide which loans you want to issue and are free to reject those that don't interest you.

There are several lending platforms you can work with. Some have restrictions on the types of people that they allow to make loans, but there are some like the LendingClub.com and Prosper.com that are open to anyone who wants to participate as long as they meet the minimum deposit requirements.

Revenue is generated by charging interest and fees to the borrowers. Some fees including origination fees, late payment fees, and others can come to as much as 6% of the loan. The fee and interest charges vary depending on the platform you use, but be prepared to see some of that money evaporate when payments come in. The lending platform will take a percentage off of every payment made for themselves before sending the balance on to you.

Why peer-to-peer lending?

For the investor, you will receive a higher yield on your money than if you left it in a savings account. It is an easy alternative to investing than stocks and bonds. You don't need a lot of knowledge to get started. You are literally free to diversify your portfolio in any direction you want. And then there is the psychological advantage of knowing that you are doing something to contribute to the advancement of society in many different ways.

Disadvantages

Unlike with financial institutions, your money is not protected by the FDIC. So, if a borrower defaults on a loan, the chances of getting your investment back is slim to none. Also, you won't be able to cash in on your investment if you need the money back before the loan matures. The average term for a loan ranges between three to five years, leaving you without access to your funds for at least that amount of time.

Because this is such a new investment instrument, there is no track record or history to refer to. New trends are being set every day, so there's no way of telling whether or not the industry will continue to be stable.

It is possible to achieve huge returns (sometimes in the double-digits) with this type of lending, but don't allow those figures to distract you from reality. It is a risky investment tool, and you should always proceed with caution.

The 10 Best Strategies for Trading Cryptocurrencies

You've most likely been living under a rock if you haven't heard of cryptocurrencies yet. This new investment tool is believed by many to be the most promising means of garnering massive amounts of money extremely fast. Today, there are probably close to 2,000 altcoins to choose from, and the number is still growing.

Bitcoin, the first and by far the most profitable of cryptocurrencies has pushed itself into the world's consciousness with a whopping rise in price that escalated from a value worth pennies when it was first released to its highest point of nearly $20,000 in December of 2017. But with so many options to choose from, a new investor could easily be overwhelmed.

While cryptocurrencies are probably the riskiest of all investment tools, it doesn't have to be that complicated. If you are brave enough to risk the highly volatile price movements and you think your heart can take the undulations of the waves, here are seven strategies that can help you get into this potentially lucrative market.

ICOs

ICOs or Initial Public Offerings can be very unpredictable because like the stock market's IPOs, these are new coins that are just getting started. When you purchase an ICO, you are literally getting in at the very beginning of a new coin. This means you're going to get the coin at a much lower price than it will be when it is released to the public. This automatically puts you in line for greater profits, sometimes as much as 2500% of your initial investment. However, because it is an entirely new coin, there is also a high risk that it will fail and take all of your money with it. Because there is no insurance protection for cryptocurrency investors, you need to do a lot of research to make sure that the team behind the coin are experienced enough to bring their new baby to life.

- Start by reviewing the list of new ICOs at https://icoranker.com/ and review the ones that interest you.

- Look for the purpose of the coin to determine its supply and demand. Coins that are designed for a limited population may not do well, but coins that have a potential to be useful for a large population can do much better.

- Once you've narrowed your list down to several viable choices, study the team members. You want to know their history, their background, their experience, and whether they can work together to meet the demands of the mission.

- Try to investigate a little further to find out what type of people are already investing in the coin. If they have a good community of investors who are optimistic about their future prospects, then you know they will support the coin and stick with it during the lean times. You can find this information by visiting the various forums set up for each coin.

- What is the legal framework between the development team and other contributors. You should find this information on the coin's whitepaper. The coin's terms and conditions should be laid out in a clear and easy to understand format.

- Visit the website and set-up an escrow wallet. You will be issued a private key you can use to sell your ICOs later.

If you decide to invest in ICOs, don't limit yourself to just one. It is easy for them to fail, so invest in several to increase your chances of success.

The best strategy for ICOs is the buy and hold strategy. The price will fluctuate wildly so don't go into a panic. Hold your coins until you see at least a 50% return on your investment before selling.

Low Price Accumulation

After a coin passes its ICO stage, it gets to join the big boys on the global marketplace. Just like with stocks, you want to buy the coins when the price is low and wait for it to go up in price. Most people will go into a panic when the price takes a significant drop, but seasoned cryptocurrency investors understand that extreme volatility is a characteristic of this type of investment.

Breakouts

By taking advantage of breakouts, you can cut down on your risks, but you need to recognize when these breakouts indicate the start of a new trend. The key to this strategy is to find the best time to enter the market by identifying areas of resistance or support that could be broken under the right conditions. In these scenarios, the coin could break through resistance upward or it can break through support and push downward.

Dollar Cost Averaging

Dollar cost averaging makes it possible for you to invest a pre-set amount of funds on a regular basis on each coin you want to buy. As a result, rather than finding the lowest or the highest price is no longer important. In essence, you are averaging out the overall cost of your coins with each payment. If done over a period of months, the prices generally come out much more favorably than if you were to make a single large payment.

Balanced

One key element in any type of investing is diversification. To successfully diversify, you need to balance your portfolio. This means investing in several different cryptos at the same time. When one coin goes into a slump you can still be earning profits on other coins.

Unbalanced

With an unbalanced strategy, investors designate a set percentage of their funds to coins based on their gut feeling about how well they expect it to perform in the future. Coins that are expected to do well are given the highest percentages while those that are not expected to perform as well will receive a lower percentage.

Profits Earned Reinvested in Other Coins

Once you've made a little money off of some cryptocurrencies, you can begin to diversify your portfolio even further by siphoning off some of your profits and investing them in new coins. By taking 50% of your earnings off of one coin and investing it in more successful coins, you can compound your success.

7 Must-Have Apps for Modern-Day Investors

Getting started in any type of investing can be tricky; even moreso for the new investor. One way to make things easier is to have a little help as you navigate all the potential pitfalls you'll face as you learn.

In the past, this kind of help was once only available to the privileged. Now, anyone can have the information available to capitalize on their growth. With the right apps to guide you, anyone can make decisions like a professional trader. Below are seven of the most effective apps all investors need to have at their disposal.

Stash

The Stash mobile app is the go-to app for investors who are looking to access the best tools for the financial market. It makes it possible for you to purchase low-cost ETFs and stocks directly from your mobile device.

The cost is only $1/month, but for that low price, you get your own investment account and are allowed to make unlimited trades, free education, and the ability to make fractional purchases of more expensive stocks with payments as low as $5.

Vault

The Vault app focuses on older investors ready for retirement. It makes it possible for them to start an individual retirement account (IRA), Roth IRA, or a SEP IRA for those who are self-employed. Investors can direct a pre-set portion of their income automatically towards the plan they choose. So, even if you don't have a retirement plan with your company, you can start investing for a low monthly fee of $1.

Personal Capital

This app gives you regular updates and keeps track of all of the investments in your portfolio. It gives you a regular evaluation of how your investments are performing and suggestions on risk management. It is even possible to quickly check for which stocks are doing the best in your portfolio and which ones you need to make adjustments to. Personal Capital also gives you a comparison of how your portfolio performance measures up against the major market indices.

Stockpile

Stockpile allows you to invest in the stock market in smaller increments. You can buy fractional shares from hundreds of different stocks for as little as $5. There is a small commission fee of

$0.99/trade, which is nominal when compared to other services that can charge as much as $10.00.

Parents or other adults can start their children off with a gift card for as little as $20. The small amount pays off in the long run as it starts the young ones off on the right foot learning money management early on.

Wealthfront

This app makes it easy to set aside cash for a college education. Users get a detailed look at their financial situation and can make investments designed to help them to appreciate their capital. You can start small and build as you go. Advice will be given based on the amount of risk you want to take and your financial goals.

E-Trade

E-Trade may seem a bit more expensive than some of the other apps, but with good reason. The app is designed so that researching and trading stocks is about as easy as it gets. You can trade stocks, ETFs, and mutual funds and get all your necessary data in real time. You can even get help in the best ways to build up your portfolio from one of their real live investment specialists.

Robinhood

The Robinhood app opens the doors to new investors by allowing them to make small trades, all commission-free. This is the perfect app if you are still a little hesitant about getting into investing. You can buy stocks, options, ETFs, and cryptocurrencies all zero fees. Their new feature, Robinhood Gold, allows you to trade after-hours and gives you a line of credit so you can make larger purchases if you qualify. There isn't much in terms of trading, research, or personal support, but the platform is simple enough to use and who can beat a no-fee service.

The world of financial investments is changing. We live in a fast-moving digital age, and with more apps like these becoming available, it is now easier than ever for new investors to step on the stage and trade just like a pro.

Conclusion

No doubt, you have discovered a lot of information here that will stir up dreams and ideas for change. Together, we've learned how to break those financial chains so you can literally find your chance at freedom.

Think about it. It doesn't matter where you start, it only matters where you finish. Even if you're so deep in debt that you can't see your way out, it is possible to navigate that maze and find your way to freedom.

It all starts with changing your mind. When you can break those mental chains that may keep you in a "safety zone" then you are free to explore profitable opportunities around every corner. Actions, positive or negative, are the result of how we view our world. If you want to change your circumstances, start by changing your mind.

After identifying the right mindset, we learned how to change your present circumstances so you can get on a better financial footing. We discovered that budgeting can be exciting and enjoyable. Instead of being just an obligation, it becomes a tool for gaining control over your money.

From there, we moved on to how to better manage your credit. After all, if you're going to be growing wealth, good credit will be an essential part of it. This is the magic recipe that could change your life and guide you in the right direction.

But, we also discussed how being financially free meant more than just getting out of debt. We can choose to continue to work for our money or we could find ways to get our money to work for us. Knowing how to invest in stocks, bonds, real estate, or other lucrative opportunities can move us to take risks that we may never have thought about before.

Imagine how your life can change if you didn't have to work for every penny you made. Instead, money just enters your life effortlessly. How awesome would that be? Your health would be better, your mental state would improve, you'd anxiety will be replaced with joy and excitement. You'd be free to spend time with your family, take vacations together, or finally turn dreams into reality.

Whether you choose to invest in the stock market or cryptocurrency, whether you want to try your hand at bonds or real estate, you now have the keys to do whatever it is that you have always wanted to do. It'll take discipline and drive, but gaining that freedom can be one of the most liberating things in your life.

You now have a map to get you to your ultimate goal of financial freedom. Use this book as your guide and refer to it often, but don't just stop there. No matter how exciting and interesting you find the advice in these pages, there is only one way they will work to benefit you, and that's to put them into practice.

Some people can get overwhelmed with this much information and try to put off taking the first step until they understand better. That could delay your chances at success indefinitely. You don't need to know every detail about the stock market to start investing. You don't need to have all the fine points down to buy real estate. All you need is the heart and the desire to make it happen.

So, go ahead — stick your toe in the water and get started. It doesn't matter if you start small, as long as you take that first step. You have the keys to your own financial freedom here. Go back through these pages, create your plan, and get going. You're already halfway there; all that's left for you to do is go for it. There is no time like the present to change your life!

www.ingramcontent.com/pod-product-compliance
Lightning Source LLC
Chambersburg PA
CBHW030324100526
44592CB00010B/557